16LIVES

MICHAEL O'HANRAHAN

CONOR KOSTICK– AUTHOR OF 16LIVES: MICHAEL O'HANRAHAN

Conor Kostick is an award-winning historian and novelist who lives in Dublin. His other historical works include *Strongbow*, *Revolution in Ireland* and, together with Lorcan Collins, *The Easter Rising – A Guide to Dublin in 1916*.

LORCAN COLLINS – SERIES EDITOR

Lorcan Collins was born and raised in Dublin. A lifelong interest in Irish history led to the foundation of his hugely popular 1916 Rebellion Walking Tour in 1996. He co-authored *The Easter Rising – A Guide to Dublin in 1916* (O'Brien Press, 2000) with Conor Kostick. His biography of James Connolly was published in the *16 Lives* series in 2012. He is also a regular contributor to radio, television and historical journals. *16 Lives* is Lorcan's concept and he is co-editor of the series.

DR RUÁN O'DONNELL – SERIES EDITOR

Dr Ruán O'Donnell is a senior lecturer at the University of Limerick. A graduate of UCD and the Australian National University, O'Donnell has published extensively on Irish Republicanism. His titles include *Robert Emmet and the Rising of 1803*; *The Impact of the 1916 Rising* (editor); *Special Category, The IRA in English Prisons 1968–1978*; and *The O'Brien Pocket History of the Irish Famine*. He is a director of the Irish Manuscripts Commission and a frequent contributor to the national and international media on the subject of Irish revolutionary history.

16 LIVES
MICHAEL O'HANRAHAN

Conor Kostick

THE O'BRIEN PRESS
DUBLIN

First published 2015 by
The O'Brien Press Ltd,
12 Terenure Road East, Rathgar, Dublin 6, D06 HD27, Ireland.
Tel: +353 1 4923333; Fax: +353 1 4922777
E-mail: books@obrien.ie. Website: www.obrien.ie

ISBN: 978-1-84717-335-5

8 7 6 5 4 3 2 1
18 17 16 15

All quotations, in English and Irish, have been reproduced with original spelling and punctuation.

Printed and bound by CPI Group (UK) Ltd, Croydon, CR0 4YY
The paper used in this book is produced using pulp from managed forests.

PICTURE CREDITS

The author and publisher thank the following for permission to use photographs and
illustrative material: front cover portrait of Michael O'Hanrahan and inside-front spread
from *A Swordman of the Brigade* courtesy of the National Library of Ireland; back cover
image of Volunteers marching courtesy of the Kilmainham Gaol Collection.

Photo section one: p1 (top and bottom), p2 (top), p3 (top and bottom), p4 (bottom left)
and p8 courtesy of the National Library of Ireland; p2 (bottom) and p4 (top) courtesy
of the Kilmainham Gaol Collection; p5 (bottom), p6, p7 (top and bottom) courtesy of
Lorcan Collins.

Photo section two: p1, p2 (top), p3 (bottom) and p4 (top) courtesy of Lorcan Collins;
p2 (bottom), p3 (top), p5 (top and bottom), p6 (top) and p7 courtesy of the Kilmainham
Gaol Collection; p4 (bottom) courtesy of the National Library of Ireland; p6 (bottom)
courtesy of the Irish Capuchin Provincial Archives, Dublin; p8 (top and bottom) courtesy
of Ray Bateson.

ACKNOWLEDGEMENTS

Heartfelt thanks are due to Clodagh Kinsella of Carlow County Libraries; Dermot Mulligan from Carlow County Museum; Niamh McDonald of the National Archives; Freya Verstraten Veach; Pat O'Neill; Valerie Bistany; Ray Bateson of the National Graves Association; Michael O'Hanrahan (no relation); Bride Roe; Pat Ingoldsby; Laura Ashcroft Jones for her diligent and eye-straining research among the newspapers of the day; and above all, to Michael Purcell, who was extremely generous with his time and who has a deep knowledge of Carlow's local history and its sources.

16LIVES Timeline

1845–51. The Great Hunger in Ireland. One million people die and over the next decades millions more emigrate.

1858, March 17. The Irish Republican Brotherhood, or Fenians, are formed with the express intention of overthrowing British rule in Ireland by whatever means necessary.

1867, February and March. Fenian Uprising.

1870, May. Home Rule movement founded by Isaac Butt, who had previously campaigned for amnesty for Fenian prisoners.

1879–81. The Land War. Violent agrarian agitation against English landlords.

1884, November 1. The Gaelic Athletic Association founded – immediately infiltrated by the Irish Republican Brotherhood (IRB).

1893, July 31. Gaelic League founded by Douglas Hyde and Eoin MacNeill. The *Gaelic Revival*, a period of Irish Nationalism, pride in the language, history, culture and sport.

1900, September. *Cumann na nGaedheal* (Irish Council) founded by Arthur Griffith.

1905–07. *Cumann na nGaedheal*, the Dungannon Clubs and the National Council are amalgamated to form *Sinn Féin* (We Ourselves).

1909, August. Countess Markievicz and Bulmer Hobson organise nationalist youths into *Na Fianna Éireann* (Warriors of Ireland) a kind of boy scout brigade.

1912, April. Asquith introduces the Third Home Rule Bill to the British Parliament. Passed by the Commons and rejected by the Lords, the Bill would have to become law due to the Parliament Act. Home Rule expected to be introduced for Ireland by autumn 1914.

1913, January. Sir Edward Carson and James Craig set up Ulster Volunteer Force (UVF) with the intention of defending Ulster against Home Rule.

1913. Jim Larkin, founder of the Irish Transport and General Workers' Union (ITGWU) calls for a workers' strike for better pay and conditions.

1913, August 31. Jim Larkin speaks at a banned rally on Sackville (O'Connell) Street; Bloody Sunday.

1913, November 23. James Connolly, Jack White and Jim Larkin establish the Irish Citizen Army (ICA) in order to protect strikers.

1913, November 25. The Irish Volunteers are founded in Dublin to 'secure the rights and liberties common to all the people of Ireland'.

1914, March 20. Resignations of British officers force British government not to use British Army to enforce Home Rule, an event known as the 'Curragh Mutiny'.

1914, April 2. In Dublin, Agnes O'Farrelly, Mary MacSwiney, Countess Constance Markievicz and others establish Cumann na mBan as a women's volunteer force dedicated to establishing Irish freedom and assisting the Irish Volunteers.

1914, April 24. A shipment of 25,000 rifles and three million rounds of ammunition is landed at Larne for the UVF.

1914, July 26. Irish Volunteers unload a shipment of 900 rifles and 45,000 rounds of ammunition shipped from Germany aboard Erskine Childers' yacht, the *Asgard*. British troops fire on crowd on Bachelor's Walk, Dublin. Three citizens are killed.

1914, August 4. Britain declares war on Germany. Home Rule for Ireland shelved for the duration of the First World War.

1914, September 9. Meeting held at Gaelic League headquarters between IRB and other extreme republicans. Initial decision made to stage an uprising while Britain is at war.

1914, September. 170,000 leave the Volunteers and form the National Volunteers or Redmondites. Only 11,000 remain as the Irish Volunteers under Eoin MacNeill.

1915, May–September. Military Council of the IRB is formed.

1915, August 1. Pearse gives fiery oration at the funeral of Jeremiah O'Donovan Rossa.

1916, January 19–22. James Connolly joins the IRB Military Council, thus ensuring that the ICA shall be involved in the Rising. Rising date confirmed for Easter.

1916, April 20, 4.15pm. *The Aud* arrives at Tralee Bay, laden with 20,000 German rifles for the Rising. Captain Karl Spindler waits in vain for a signal from shore.

1916, April 21, 2.15am. Roger Casement and his two companions go ashore from U-19 and land on Banna Strand in Kerry. Casement is arrested at McKenna's Fort.

6.30pm. *The Aud* is captured by the British navy and forced to sail towards Cork harbour.

1916, 22 April, 9.30am. *The Aud* is scuttled by her captain off Daunt Rock.

10pm. Eoin MacNeill as chief-of-staff of the Irish Volunteers issues the countermanding order in Dublin to try to stop the Rising.

1916, April 23, 9am, Easter Sunday. The Military Council of the Irish Republican Brotherhood (IRB) meets to discuss the situation, since MacNeill has placed an advertisement in a Sunday newspaper halting all Volunteer operations. The Rising is put on hold for twenty-four hours. Hundreds of copies of *The Proclamation of the Irish Republic* are printed in Liberty Hall.

1916, April 24, 12 noon, Easter Monday. The Rising begins in Dublin.

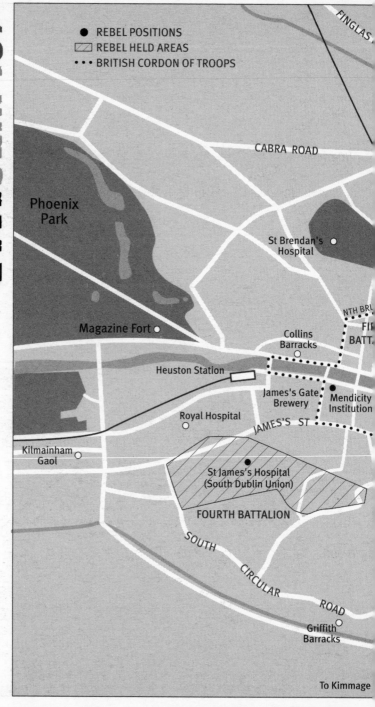

16 LIVES MAP

- ● REBEL POSITIONS
- ▨ REBEL HELD AREAS
- ••• BRITISH CORDON OF TROOPS

FINGLAS

CABRA ROAD

Phoenix Park

St Brendan's Hospital

NTH BRL

FIR
BATT.

Magazine Fort

Collins Barracks

Heuston Station

James's Gate Brewery

Mendicity Institution

Royal Hospital

JAMES'S ST

Kilmainham Gaol

St James's Hospital (South Dublin Union)

FOURTH BATTALION

SOUTH

CIRCULAR

ROAD

Griffith Barracks

To Kimmage

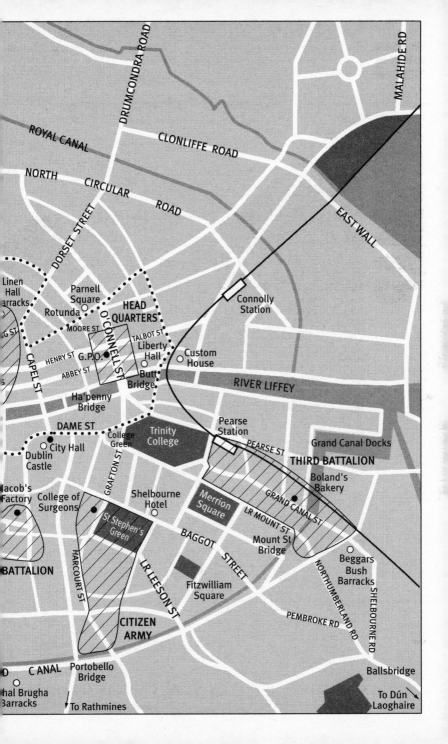

16LIVES – Series Introduction

This book is part of a series called *16 LIVES*, conceived with the objective of recording for posterity the lives of the sixteen men who were executed after the 1916 Easter Rising. Who were these people and what drove them to commit themselves to violent revolution?

The rank and file as well as the leadership were all from diverse backgrounds. Some were privileged and some had no material wealth. Some were highly educated writers, poets or teachers and others had little formal schooling. Their common desire, to set Ireland on the road to national freedom, united them under the one banner of the army of the Irish Republic. They occupied key buildings in Dublin and around Ireland for one week before they were forced to surrender. The leaders were singled out for harsh treatment and all sixteen men were executed for their role in the Rising.

Meticulously researched yet written in an accessible fashion, the *16 LIVES* biographies can be read as individual volumes but together they make a highly collectible series.

Lorcan Collins & Dr Ruán O'Donnell,
16 Lives *Series Editors*

CONTENTS

Chapter 1

• • • • •

1846–1898

The Corkcutter

… while tinmen's shops, and noisy trunk-makers,
Knife-grinders, coopers, squeaking cork-cutters,
Fruit-barrows, and the hunger-giving cries
Of vegetable-vendors, fill the air.
'London's Summer Morning', Mary Darby Robinson (1800)

In the mid-nineteenth century the corkcutting trade in Ireland was in the hands of a very small number of master craftsmen, one of whom was Richard O'Hanrahan of New Ross. Because of the bulky nature of cork, those who practised the trade of converting the bark of the Mediterranean tree into finished goods generally lived in a port; Richard, who was born in 1846 and grew up in one of Ireland's major ports, Wexford, found in the late 1860s that he could make a living at the equally busy *entrepôt* of New Ross. New Ross at the time was home to about 5,000 people, many of whom were employed in connection with the vigorous trade that arrived at the town's long stretch of quays. Ships – schooners under sail more often than steam-powered vessels – would arrive there with timber, coal, manures, lace, boots and other cargoes. They would depart with bacon, beer, felt, leather and the goods of smaller industries.[1] And there too, the shipments of cork would arrive, typically from Portugal, and be delivered to Richard's workshop.

One of the reasons for Richard's move from Wexford – via a number of other brief addresses – to New Ross was that he felt under pressure from the British authorities. Earlier in the 1860s Richard had been sworn in as a member of the Irish Republican Brotherhood, the secret organisation also known as the Fenians, which, under the influence of its main organiser, James Stephens, strove for an independent Irish republic and, indeed, a republic for the poor.[2]

With the main IRB leaders having been arrested in 1865, and with informers having a heavy presence in the movement, an effort to launch an uprising against British rule early in 1867 stalled badly. The IRB consequently suffered further from the capture and the execution of those involved in planning the rising. This, and the subsequent atmosphere of repression, may have provided the context for Richard's departure from Wexford. In leaving home, he left a supportive family, including his brother, Watty O'Hanrahan, who had a large printing business in the town.[3]

Having survived the danger of arrest and having established a business in New Ross, by 1870 – although a youthful twenty-four and of modest means – Richard felt confident enough in his future to invite nineteen-year-old Mary Williams to come from Wexford and marry him. Mary was a sister of John Williams, the chief accountant in Cherry's Brewery and it might well have been that Mary met Richard through the brewery's employment of O'Hanrahan as a corkcutter.[4]

Living in one of a row of houses that made up St Mary's Terrace (off South Street) and then in Barrack Lane, the young couple's early efforts to start a family were met with tragedy when their first two babies, both called Richard, died at or near birth in March 1871 and March 1872 in New Ross.[5] Their next attempt at having a child saw Mary travel home to Wexford in 1875 for the labour, and this time they were rewarded with the successful birth of the first of three sons: Henry ('Harry' to his family and friends). In 1877, Michael was delivered in New Ross, followed by Edward, also in New Ross, in 1879.[6]

Born on 16 January 1877, Michael O'Hanrahan was baptised in the old parish church, now St Michael's Theatre, South Street. Two of Mary's cousins acted as his godmother and godfather, suggesting that the closer relatives of the young family were not to hand. It is probable that their nearest family was still in Wexford, as that is where Mary went for support for the birth of Henry.[7]

A plaque dedicated to Michael's memory on the Tholsel building in New Ross offers the highly symbolic date of 17 March as his birthday, and a number of publications and websites have made St Patrick's Day Michael's birthday ever since. But the evidence of the birth certificate supports the January date.[8]

The surname that Michael carried was inherited from the O'h-Anraghain dynasty of pre-Norman Irish lords: not necessarily by direct birthright, as the lower social orders of the land often took their surnames from their princes. The name appears in connection with aristocrats in Corcaraidhe (a territory in the county of Westmeath, later forming the barony of Corcaree) and O'h-Anraghain nobles also had a presence in a district in County Tipperary. In the 1659 poll-tax returns, the family name was most common in Limerick County and to a lesser extent, Tipperary and Sligo.[9]

In Michael's day, the surname had been anglicised in three common forms: O'Hanraghan, O'Hanrahan and Hanrahan. As an adult, Michael preferred to use the Gaelic *Ua hAnnracáin*. Of those who bore the name in previous centuries, perhaps the most illustrious was Mulbrennan O'h-Anraghain (d. 1132), abbot of Clonfert. Another O'h-Anraghain of note was the priest Daniel O'Hanraghan, who as an elderly man was killed by English soldiers at Lislaughtin, County Kerry, on 6 April 1580.[10]

The young family's departure from New Ross, *c.*1880,

came about because Corcoran's Mineral Water Factory in Carlow Town needed a corker on site to cut stoppers for products such as Corcoran's red lemonade, seltzer water, soda water, aromatic ginger ale, ginger beer and champagne cider.[11] Established in 1827 by Thomas Corcoran, the company had flourished to become one of Carlow's major employers. As the job offered Richard a steady income, he acquired a house in the town and soon saved enough to set up on his own with Corcoran's as his main customer. In 1881, the family moved to 90 and 91 Tullow Street, a house, shop and workshop on a major thoroughfare of Carlow Town. All along Tullow Street were represented the main trades of the era: butchers, tanners, shoemakers, ironmongers, timber makers, jewellers, glassworkers, painters and decorators, bakers, coach builders, dressmakers, drapers, blacksmiths, malters, grocers, dyers and printers.[12] Number 90, where the O'Hanrahans lived, evidenced the progress of Richard's career: it was made of stone with a sturdy roof and four windows facing the street. The house had five rooms, one of them the shop.[13]

At the time, the Carlow location was an effective one for serving businesses in Dublin. While the tolls on the Grand Canal that connected Carlow to Dublin were expensive, small bags of corks could be easily transported to the capital by horse and cart and – increasingly – by rail. The Great Southern and Western Railway's line from Dublin to Kilkenny via Carlow was constructed between 1846 and 1850, while the Bagenalstown and Wexford Railway serving Borris was begun in 1855. Supplies of the bark that was his raw material could reach Richard's new workshop easily enough via the River Barrow, which joined the Suir to reach the sea at Waterford, a city with a small corkcutting industry of its own.

Like the country as a whole, County Carlow was still suffering in the aftermath of the Great Famine of the 1840s. The population had dropped from 86,000 in 1841 to 52,000 in 1871, at which time the decline had still not stabilised. The 'push' factor of the famine years had been followed by a 'pull' factor as the generation of emigrants who had settled in the USA, Canada, Australia, etc., invited their relatives to follow them. In 1881, the population of County Carlow was down to 47,000 and in 1901 it was just 38,000, less than half of what it had been sixty years previously. Outside of the major cities, this trend, unfortunately, was more or less the same across Ireland. Carlow Town had suffered slightly less than the countryside, but even so, the urban population fell from 10,409 in 1841 to 6,513 in 1901.[14]

Once settled in Tullow Street, Mary had another baby, Richard (b. 1881), who died before his first birthday.[15] Soon, however, three daughters joined the family. The 1901 census lists Anna (b. 1884), Mary (b. 1887) and Eillen (b. 1889). Mary would be known to all as Máire and Eillen as Eily. In addition, the O'Hanrahans had room to take on lodgers and in 1901, brothers Dominic and James Dillon, a carpenter and a wheeler, were also living in 90 Tullow Street.[16]

It is possible to discern two of the values that were highly thought of in the O'Hanrahan household. Education was clearly prized, with all of the children being able to compete for white-collar jobs. At the time of the 1901 census, Anna, aged seventeen, was a stationer, while Edward had won a place in the Post Office as a sorting clerk and telegraphist. Harry and Michael were practising the corkcutter's trade, yet not only had they learned Irish by this time but they had also acquired precise and accurate literacy and numeracy skills. Harry and Michael – when not working full-time for revolution – would go on to work in insurance (Harry), and as a fundraiser, proofreader in Irish, journalist and novelist (Michael).

The other strong family value was republicanism. Not only was Richard a Fenian, but the family also kept alive the memory of a near relative who, at the age of seventeen, participated in the uprising of the United Irishmen, joining the noted leader Fr John Murphy in the battle of Oulart Hill on 27 May 1798 before returning to his home by the River Slaney months later.[17] Richard's rebel past seems to have been an important influence on his children, with Harry, Michael and Eily in particular playing a very committed role in the fight for Irish independence. During the Civil War, Harry and Eily took an anti-Treaty position, which seems to reflect the more plebeian republicanism of their father; it certainly went against the views of the IRB leadership of 1922, who backed the Treaty. More definite evidence for a strong belief in social justice in the O'Hanrahan household is the participation of Harry and Michael in the creation of Carlow's Workingman's Club.

Life at the O'Hanrahans' in Tullow Street would have been completely coloured by the scents and sounds of corkcutting. This was a trade that was mainly concerned with the supply of corks for bottles and earthenware jars. The demand for new corks in Ireland was not for wine: people would keep their old corks for that purpose. Rather, it came from brewers to cap their beer bottles (until the invention of the crown cap) and from grocers and farmers for fruit, pickle and sauce jars, etc. Corks were also required for certain drinks, such as ginger beer and lemonade. Shoemakers, too, would sometimes work with cork insoles. Somewhat more specialised handcrafted corkcutting was needed to produce swimming aids, floats for fishing nets and discs for machines in the cutglass industry. There was also a small demand for bath mats and components in hats and bustles.

Having collected their cargo of Mediterranean bark, Richard and the boys would take it to the back yard for burning. One of the important properties of cork is its fire resistance, which allows for the outside of the bark to be burned so that the cork shrinks, its pores close and it becomes fully waterproof without the flames consuming the whole. Turning the bark in the fire with a minimum of waste was the most skilled job of the corkcutter and was usually performed by the master, in this case Richard. By contrast, brushing off the ash was a filthy job given to the apprentices, i.e. the boys. The ash (along with all the small, unworkable pieces of cork) was saved for sale to dyers, being a valuable ingredient for the creation of pigments for dark colours. When the scorched outer layer of bark was cut off (some twenty-four hours after the burning process), a strip remained, which was cut into quarters, and from these were cut the finished products.

Cutting hundreds and hundreds of cork items was boring work, but there were advantages to practising this trade compared to some of the other work being carried out on Tullow Street. In winter, the O'Hanrahan house would have been warm as a result of the burning process. There was no seasonality to the demand for cork products, so the household income would be fairly steady the whole year round. Also, other than the characteristic squeaking sound of the knife working the cork, it was a relatively quiet trade, so the family could sit and converse while working.

The great problem the family had to face, however, was that in Ireland and elsewhere theirs was a trade in decline; or rather, the small home workshop was on its way to becoming extinct, being replaced by the factory. The peak years for the – always small – spread of the corkcutting industry were the 1860s, after which it became more centralised. Not only were inventions like the glass bottle stopper removing some of the demand for local corkcutters (and this would eventually affect the O'Hanrahan's main customer, Corcoran's), but machine processes were revolutionising the trade. As the *Birmingham Daily Post* noted in 1891, 'a skillful corkcutter can produce from 1,500 to 2,000 corks a day, his only tools being two sharp knives with broad blades. Machines have been made which can cut 2,000 an hour.'[18] Moreover, in 1894 Henry Avern and a member of the Barris family from Palafrugell in Spain built a factory in Silves, Portugal, that employed hundreds of corkcutters, in contrast to the industry average of workshops with just five workers.[19] Giving the children other career options through education, then, was not only a worthy aspiration; it was a necessity. And over the long century from the birth of Henry in 1875 to the death of Máire in 1975, it has to be recognised that the shadow of poverty was a constant presence over the children of the corkcutter.

The boys of the O'Hanrahan household attended the local Christian Brothers School, at that time on College Street, near Carlow Cathedral.[20] Here, their enthusiasm for the national cause would not have suffered at all; in all likelihood it was encouraged. Among the many students who attended the school and subsequently became involved in the national struggle was Padraig Mac Gamhna (Paddy Gaffney), a radical socialist republican to whom – coincidentally – a plaque is dedicated at number 92 Tullow Street, his former residence.

After attending the Christian Brothers School, Michael planned to take the examination for a place in the Civil Service. But on learning that all civil servants were required to take an oath of allegiance to the Queen, he abandoned that goal. According to Eily, he told Richard and Mary, 'I will never earn or take a penny of English money.' 'His decision,' she recalled, 'was valiantly upheld by my parents.'[21] After leaving school, Michael and Harry worked in their family business, while Edward – who did not object to its Imperial shortcomings – entered the Post Office. But their education was not complete, for all the children in the family set about the task of learning Irish, with the most passionate for the language being Michael.

Chapter 2

1898

The Language Enthusiast

Although his determination not to train for a role in the Imperial administration demonstrates that Michael O'Hanrahan had a nationalist outlook from an early age, his first step towards being an organiser for the Easter Rising came with his joining the Gaelic League on 4 March 1898, at the age of twenty-one. There was no necessary connection, of course, between learning the Irish language and becoming a revolutionary, a point that the Gaelic League founders themselves made clear in the first issue of the *Gaelic Journal* in 1882. There, they made the observation (quoting an article in the London *Times*) that the artificial cultivation of the Irish language would create no obstacle to the political amalgamation of Ireland with the Empire.[1] This was a declaration of innocent intent and non-confrontation by the relatively conservative editorial board. But their obsequious prediction was proven quite wrong. Many men and women developed a radical form of national politics after having first devoted their energies to saving the Irish language. As Patrick Pearse put it in 1914: 'I think I am right in holding that the Volunteer movement has sprung out of the language movement. It is one of a large and thriving family of youngsters of whom, whether it own them or not (and it is chary enough about owning some of them), the Gaelic League is undoubtedly the parent. The League has become a highly respectable member of society: it sits in high places and has cultured leisure. But it will be recognised in history as the most revolutionary influence that has ever come into Ireland.'[2]

Michael O'Hanrahan was an early adherent of the Gaelic League, whose formal beginning was at a meeting initiated by the Church of Ireland Trinity scholar Douglas Hyde on 31 July 1893. Having joined within five years of its creation, O'Hanrahan was an unusual member of the Gaelic League in regard to his youth and his relatively modest social circumstances, and also in his being among the minority of language enthusiasts who were based outside of Dublin. The Gaelic League's initial activity was very much focused on the capital.

There was very little support for the study of the Irish language unless from the Gaelic League and it took that organisation nearly a decade to begin funding regional teachers.

For those without access to a teacher, the classic text to study was Fr Eugene O'Growney's *Simple Lessons in Irish,* which was first published as a series in the *Weekly Freeman* and became widely available in Ireland after assembly in booklet form by MH Gill & Son in 1894. There were five books in the set, of increasing difficulty, and by 1903, 320,000 copies had been sold.[3]

Whether through O'Growney or other means, Michael and Harry attained a 'considerable knowledge of Irish, through their own unaided efforts'.[4] So successful was Michael in his efforts to master Irish that his proficiency qualified him to teach classes on behalf of the Gaelic League. Much of this study must have been at home and independently motivated, for when he joined the Gaelic League, there was no branch in Carlow. In 1917, republican priest Fr Michael O'Flanagan wrote a preface to one of Michael's works at the request of the family. In it, he explained that Michael's 'knowledge of Irish was acquired entirely in Gaelic League classes and by private study. The earnestness with which he always gave himself up to the work at hand was here exemplified. He often remained up until two or three o'clock in the morning mastering his Irish grammar and text books.'[5]

The subject of the Irish language was one that had the power to stir Michael deeply and a description of him in his twenties was of 'a placid, gentle, earnest young man in whom the writer's gift was gradually developing, and who, speaking slowly and distinctly in debate, had always something to say that was worth hearing and remembering. It was only when some thoughtless or mischievous speaker belittled the Irish language and Irish history and Irish games, saying we could be very good Irishmen speaking English only and playing Soccer or Rugby, if only we had political freedom, it was only then that placidity and calmness deserted Micheál O hAnnracháin. His face became deadly pale and his voice trembled with the anger he tried to repress as he lashed the slavishness that would be content with such bogus independence.'[6]

From 1851, the Irish census figures included information about the Irish language, and from them, some idea of the challenge facing Michael O'Hanrahan and the Gaelic League becomes evident. The 1851 figures (perhaps under-reporting the use of Irish) show that 233 people in every 1,000 could speak Irish, but that use of the language was diminishing among the young. Among children under ten, only 11.4 percent of boys and 10.5 percent of girls could speak Irish. By 1891, the decline in the use of the language was evident in the fact that out of every 1,000 people, only 145 could speak Irish; moreover, the fact that only 3.1 percent of children under ten spoke the language pointed towards its near-extinction over the next generation.

These were welcome figures from the perspective of the British government, whose attitude was that expressed by

English poet Edmund Spenser in the sixteenth century: 'The speech being Irish, the heart must needs be Irish.' In other words, the authorities viewed with suspicion those still using the language. Irish speakers were shut out of the legal system, whose documents were entirely in English. Indeed, even writing your name in Irish was to risk prosecution. In 1905, for example, Patrick Pearse went before three judges to defend Niall Mac Giolla Brighde of Creeslough in Donegal, who was taken to court for having his name in Irish only (and in Irish script) on his cart. Not only was it agreed that this was an offence, but a later case determined that writing the Irish form of names in Roman lettering was also a crime.[7]

In 1912, Cork Gaelic League organiser Peadar Ó hAnnracháin (no relation to Michael) was arrested for giving his name and address to the police in Irish. At the trial, Chairman J Woulfe Flanagan told Ó hAnnracháin that he was obliged, if he had an English name, to give it when asked by the police. When challenged, Woulfe Flanagan cited cases such as that of Mac Giolla Brighde. In reply, Ó hAnnracháin entertained the public gallery by saying that the law only applied to carts and vehicles, 'and he was neither one or the other'. While Woulfe Flanagan wanted to convict Ó hAnnracháin, the two other – local – justices voted to drop the case.[8]

Such hostility by the authorities to the use of the Irish language played a part in politicising those who wished to speak and write it. And in the early years of the twentieth century, Michael O'Hanrahan kept company with hundreds of other men and women moving along a trajectory of involvement with the Gaelic League to support for Sinn Féin and then the Volunteers. This evolution of O'Hanrahan's political thinking was reinforced through contact with the leading national figures of the movement, which took place soon after the inauguration of a Carlow branch of the Gaelic League.

It takes a certain kind of boldness in regard to a belief in the possibility of change, as well as a supportive milieu, to create lasting new organisations where none previously existed. The fact that O'Hanrahan and his friends founded the Carlow branch of the Gaelic League testifies to his political creativity and self-belief, as well as his passion for the language.

A minimum of seven members were required to create a branch of the Gaelic League, and on 4 March 1898 the organisation was launched in Carlow. A month later, Michael wrote a report to the national organisation, which was read to their weekly meeting.

> Carlow Gaelic Class. The Irish Class formed in Carlow on March 4th, 1898 is going ahead very well. It is held temporarily in the Commercial Club, Dublin-street, but at the last meeting of the class a deputation was appointed to wait on the Rev J. Cullen, Adm. to request the use of the

Institute. The three following new members were elected at last meeting, held on 24th March – Messrs. W. O'Neill, J. O'Neill, and Mr McMahon. The books used are Father O'Growney's *Simple Lessons,* Part I. in which the members show good progress. The subscription has been fixed at 2d. per week. We are confident that a glorious future awaits the Irish language in Carlow ... Six of our members subscribe to *Fáinne an Lae* – M. O h-Annracáin.[9]

The hoped-for rooms in the Institute, College Street, soon materialised (by 16 April 1898) and initially, classes met from 7.30pm to 9pm on Mondays and Thursdays, with Michael O'Hanrahan the organiser for those wishing to join.[10] The flavour of those meetings survives thanks to a note by Tom Little, President of the Typographical Association: 'I attended the Irish classes in the Institute on Sunday last, 19th February, 1899 and spent a very enjoyable two hours. There was a good attendance. Johney Kavanagh recited, "Michael Dwyer", and "the Dialogue between the Welshman and the Irishman", and then sang, "God Save Ireland", in Irish. Harry O'Hanrahan sang "The Croppy Boy", in English. Michael O'Hanrahan gave some readings and finished up the night by singing "The Memory of the Dead", in Irish.'[11]

Fáinne an Lae ('Dawning of the Day'), the newspaper that published Michael's report of the founding meeting in Carlow, was a risky commercial venture by Brian Ó Dubhghaill (Bernard Doyle) of Upper Ormond Quay, Dublin.

Son of a compositor who had been jailed for printing Fenian literature, Bernard invested in the manufacture of a hard movable type necessary for printing a newspaper in Irish script, and from its first number on 8 January 1898 *Fáinne an Lae* appeared as a semi-official voice of the Gaelic League. In Carlow, Michael O'Hanrahan was keen to develop support for the new journal, whose appearance might well have provided the impetus for his initiative in founding a branch.

In return, Michael's practical and down-to-earth strategy for creating the Carlow branch of the Gaelic League might have contributed an important case study to the subsequent *Fáinne an Lae* editorial: 'How to Start a Gaelic League'.

So many inquiries reach *Fáinne an Lae* from time to time asking how the writer should set about forming a Gaelic League, that it seems desirable to make a few remarks on this matter. These remarks must necessarily be of a very general character, but the earnest inquirer can easily ascertain for himself the necessary details by writing to two or three Gaelic Leagues that seem to be circumstanced like his own, and asking how they do things. He will find that he has friends everywhere willing to give him a hand if he is himself in earnest.

There are two methods of starting a Gaelic League. One is to call together a number of people of position and influence, taking special care to select persons who neither know nor care anything about the language, but are ready to make speeches on that or any other subject that may bring them a little notoriety. This is the great deadhead policy and is very useful for getting the names of the promoters of the meeting into the newspapers. As a Gaelic League built upon such a foundation of sand is pretty sure to crumble away in a few months at most, no great harm is done unless, perhaps, there are a few earnest people in the locality who wish to found a genuine Gaelic League and find their efforts discounted by the failure of the big show. The other and commonsense method is for two or three genuine lovers of the language to come together and, if possible, to induce a few other real workers, or, at least, real sympathisers, to join them. There then is a Gaelic League already formed without speechifying, regulations, promotion money, or any of the thousand-and-one bits of red tape with which it is so easy to strangle real endeavour. Later on, perhaps, when the membership increases it may be necessary to make some rules, to fix subscriptions or to appoint officers among whom the growing volume of work can be divided. But, in the beginning, it is more profitable to do some work than to formulate rules which at best are of no value unless to keep troublesome members in order.[12]

The Gaelic League was a very heterodox organisation with a membership that ran across all social strata, involving both men and women, young and old. But having made this observation, it can also be demonstrated that the appeal of the Irish language movement, while broad, had its biases. Between 1893 and 1910, 85 percent of the members and 90 percent of the executive of the Gaelic League were male; the mean age of the membership was 32.6 years; and from 1894–99 there were no semi-skilled or unskilled members, with only 5 percent being from the lower middle class, i.e. skilled artisans, clerks, junior civil servants, teachers, shop assistants, etc.[13] Many people of this last milieu were to become involved in advanced nationalism in Ireland in its various forms, and (in alliance with a small section of the working class) it was overwhelmingly this stratum of Irish society that provided the fighters for the Easter Rising.

Because of the high profile of well-to-do leaders of the Gaelic League – such as the Trinity College academic Douglas Hyde – and because it did not have a strong following among the lowest strata of Irish society, the Gaelic League could be portrayed by contemporaries as a movement of the elite. Thus, from Sean O'Casey: 'These respectable, white-collared, trim-suited Gaelic Leaguers, snug in their selected branches, living rosily in Whitehall, Drumcondra, Rathgar, Donnybrook, and all the other nicer habitations of the city.'[14] And sometimes the Gaelic League itself had representatives who furthered such a view. When, in 1901, Mary Butler wrote a piece for the Gaelic League, 'Women's Role in Sustaining Gaelic Culture', she revealed how the perspective of some of those in the movement was unconsciously orientated towards the wealthy when she urged members to 'employ Irish-speaking servants whenever possible'.[15]

The first Carlow branch of the Gaelic League was younger and more plebeian than was typical for the organisation, and may indeed have been the first artisan-based branch in the country. For it was not until November 1900 that the Ard Craobh [Central Branch] of the Gaelic League wrote to encourage Trades Councils to become involved in the movement. There was subsequently some success among the trades, with, for example, the Metropolitan Housepainters Union forming a branch in 1900 and Dublin printers creating a branch in 1901. In 1910, the radical trade union of the unskilled, the Irish Transport and General Workers' Union (ITGWU), had a contingent on the annual procession in support of the Irish language. It did so again in 1911, when (controversially) the syndicalist revolutionary and leader of the ITGWU, Jim Larkin, spoke on an official platform.[16]

In setting up the branch, Michael and Harry O'Hanrahan went to 'the Commercial Young Men of Carlow'.[17] An examination of the census shows that the Gaelic League in Carlow arose from the interest in the Irish language among the young men of a few trades. The professions that can be identified in regard to the other regular members of Carlow's Gaelic League branch *c.*1898 are: James Breen (34), printer and compositor;[18] John Doyle (37), accountant, wool merchant and victualler;[19] William Ellis (27), printer and compositor;[20] Thomas White (31), gardener;[21] John Conlan (36), journalist;[22] and Thomas Lillis (34), national teacher.[23] In all probability the branch had women members too, to judge from the fact that the three O'Hanrahan sisters all had Irish by 1901 and by 1904 a Mrs Whyte was on the committee. In 1911, Mary O'Hanrahan, writing as Máire Ní hAnnracáin, had a prize-winning essay in Irish published in the radical nationalist newspaper *Irish Freedom*.[24]

Although only twenty-one and by far the youngest of his peers, Michael was elected by them as secretary of the Carlow Gaelic League, in which capacity he soon entered into the life of the national organisation and encountered other people on the same journey towards revolution as himself, most notably Patrick Pearse.[25] Having launched the Gaelic League in Carlow and arranged its language classes, the following month Michael O'Hanrahan undertook the first of many journeys to Dublin to meet other officers of the Gaelic League. At a well-attended assembly of the Ard Craobh in Dublin, on Friday 8 April 1898, in the rooms of 24 Upper O'Connell Street, Michael met Patrick Pearse, who was in the chair. And if the young man up from the country was reluctant to come forward, his natural quietness of manner did not prevent Michael from rendering a version of 'Eibhlín a Rúin' in the singing that followed the meeting's business.[26]

Like very many branches of the Gaelic League, attendance at the Carlow branch rose and fell sharply. Just two months after the foundation of the branch, Michael found it necessary to attempt to galvanise interest in its activities through a letter to *The Nationalist and Leinster Times.*

11 May, 1898

Dear Sir – It is strange the disgraceful apathy which exists in Carlow and district with regard to the gallant struggle being waged for the preservation of the Irish language as the National language of Ireland. The people of Carlow, lay and cleric, seem to be sunk in profound slumber with regard to this great question. Every little question, no matter what its interest to Irishmen, has its advocates in this town, while they seem to shun this greatest of questions as if it were plague. Let them remember that if the Irish language is allowed to perish the life of the Irish Nation as a separate nation ceases. Let them remember also that with the Irish people of the present generation rests the honour of saving or the disgrace of losing the Gaelic language. It is a disgrace to the town of Carlow that a class of even ten cannot be got together on any night. Throughout Europe at the present time every scholar of any note possesses a knowledge of the Irish language and in all the great universities of the world there are chairs of Irish. And surely when these men take up the study of Irish, men living in the heart of holy Ireland, the land of saints and sages, will not be more backward. If the Irish language is allowed to die the Irish people as a separate nation cannot long exist. With its departure most of the Irish games, customs and aspirations shall depart, and the powerful wave of Anglicization having nothing to stem its course will gradually forge its way into the very heart of the country, and Ireland will become a mere English province. Preserve the Irish language and you take the most effectual means of stemming this torrent of Anglicization and thus preserve the Irish Nation. Yours, etc., in the cause of the Irish language, M. O'Hanrahan.

In 1898 then, it appeared to Michael (and he was far from being the only one who held this view, to judge by the many articles in *Fáinne an Lae* and later in *An Claidheamh Soluis* to the same effect) that there was a real danger of Ireland becoming so integrated into the culture of the Empire as to quell all hope of independence. In that light, the struggle to learn the language was an intensely political one, despite the protestations to the contrary of some of the League's leadership. Later events were to show that Ireland could, in fact, win its freedom from British rule while the vast majority of the people used English as their first language. In its day, however, Michael's letter was appropriately pitched to motivate those who wanted to see an independent Ireland into making the effort to learn

Irish. His argument might have been effective, too, but for the emergence of a whole new outlet for nationalist feeling.

If your main reason for learning Irish *c.*1900 was to defy British rule, then at exactly the same time as Michael O'Hanrahan set up the local branch of the Gaelic League a new campaign came into being in Carlow and across the country that offered an even more promising route towards the same goal. A major initiative that might well have drawn energy away from the first Gaelic League branch in Carlow arose from the fast-approaching centenary of the uprising of the United Irishmen. Back on the morning of 25 May 1798, a terrible massacre had been carried out in Carlow when supporters of the United Irishmen had been lured into an ambush in the centre of the town; in the ensuing carnage, some six hundred men died. A mass grave at 'Croppy Hole' in the suburb of Graigue held the remains of the dead, along with the bodies of dozens of subsequent victims who afterwards were tortured and hung on the word of informers.

Reflecting the split in the elite nationalist movement at the time (between supporters of Parnell, now led by John Redmond, and opponents of Parnell, in the Irish Party), there were two commemoration committees in Carlow: the Redmondite '98 Memorial Club and the Irish Party's Commemoration Committee. The young O'Hanrahan brothers preferred the followers of John Redmond. Harry attended the '98 Memorial Club as an ordinary member (it being a Thursday night, Michael was at language classes), where he seconded a motion to withdraw the '98 Memorial GAA football team from a local tournament after a massive sprawling fight at a match at the end of April. This was the second time in a decade that a football club in Carlow had to be disbanded due to rioting.[27]

The rival commemoration organisations were prevailed upon to unite, and on Thursday 26 May 1898 at 9pm, the first of two major marches in Carlow took place when about 5,000 people turned out to honour the fallen. The route took them around Barrack Street, Tullow Street – where the O'Hanrahans would have been one of several families to illuminate their houses for the occasion – along Coal Market and through Chapel Street and Graigue to 'Croppy Hole'. 'As a popular demonstration,' reported *The Nationalist and Leinster Times*, 'nothing like the one under notice has been witnessed for many years in Carlow.'[28] Hundreds of people from Carlow then travelled that Sunday, 29 May, on a special train to Enniscorthy in County Wexford to assemble with the 15,000 who made up the crowds on Vinegar Hill, where John Redmond was the main speaker.[29] On Sunday 24 July another massive commemoration demonstration 'numbering almost every man who has put his hand to local National work within the past two decades', saw the unveiling of a memorial at 'Croppy Hole'.[30]

This revived enthusiasm for the national struggle brought

Michael O'Hanrahan into contact with Michael Governey, a very significant figure in Carlow. Having married Thomas Corcoran's daughter, Eliza, Governey inherited the mineral water business in 1876. It was he who came to an agreement with Richard O'Hanrahan to supply corks for his factory and who now, aged forty-five, was the leading supporter of John Redmond in Carlow. Governey was the main Carlow speaker at the various commemoration events; he was also the Chair of the Town Commission and a steward at the annual Carlow Races.

It proved possible for Michael O'Hanrahan and Michael Governey to work together in a number of organisations in Carlow, most notably the Gaelic League. But this apparent comradeship belied fundamentally differing political out-looks — reflecting the post-1916 division between the supporters of John Redmond and the supporters of Sinn Féin — a difference that would result in the fact that while rebels were in Kilmainham Jail in 1916 awaiting execution, Michael Governey as Chairperson was leading Carlow Council in moving a motion 'to assist the authorities as far as in our power to eradicate now, and forever the element of disorder in Ireland'.[31] Colleagues in 1898, Governey and O'Hanrahan were on opposite sides of the barricades in 1916.

Chapter 3

• • • • •

1899

The Local Organiser

Ayear after its formation, the Carlow branch of the Gaelic League faltered, and Michael found it necessary to organise a relaunch, this time with the assistance of the Catholic Church and the Redmondites. While consciously a non-sectarian organisation, and while often encountering mistrust, if not hostility, from sceptical members of the Catholic Church, the Gaelic League was very willing to avail of the infrastructure of the Church to assist its classes. For its part, the hierarchy was positively inclined towards the Gaelic League after both organisations agreed upon a call for bilingualism in Ireland's schools. The number of Gaelic League branches with priests as presidents jumped from around 50 percent in the first years of the League's existence to around 70 percent in 1900. In this regard, Carlow was in step with national developments, and on 18 March 1899, Michael O'Hanrahan and the local clergy promoted a revived branch of the Gaelic League.

The Carlow branch, which has been lately revived, is held in the Institute, College-street, which has been again kindly given by the Rev J. Cullen, Adm. Mr J. Kavanagh, who was till lately a teacher of the Tralee branch, is teacher. Class nights are Monday, Wednesday and Friday evenings, from 8 o'clock till 10 o'clock. At present the attendance is not very large, but we hope to receive a larger amount of support after Dr Hickey, of Maynooth, gives his lecture in the Town Hall, and which takes place on March 13th, at 8 o'clock. This lecture has been promoted by the respected Adm., Rev J. Cullen, who is working very energetically for its success. The Rev Dr Murphy, P.P., Kildare, a good Irish scholar, will preside.[1]

The public meeting by the recently appointed Chair of Irish at Maynooth, Michael O'Hickey, was indeed a great success that brought the branch back to its feet, as *An Claidheamh Soluis* reported:

The Carlow branch realized £10 on the lecture lately delivered by the Rev Dr Hickey on *The Tongue of the Gael*. At the conclusion of the lecture Mr Paul A. Brown, Solicitor, proposed and Mr Wm. Byrne seconded the adoption of the following resolutions, which were carried unanimously:

1. 'That this meeting urges the importance of reviving, preserving, and perpetuating the Irish language on national, educational, and philological grounds.'

2. 'To show our approval of the Gaelic League, we hereby

establish a branch in Carlow, and promise to support the organ of the Gaelic League.'

3. 'That we hereby call on all representative men on County, District and Urban Councils to forward the interests of the Irish language movement.'

4. 'That we recommend Irish be taught in all educational institutions throughout the country.'[2]

And:

On the Sunday, following Dr Hickey's lecture, a meeting was held in the Town Hall, for the purpose of selecting officers for the branch. There was a good attendance. The following officers were selected: President, Rev J. Cullen, Administrator; Vice-President, Rev Fr Lalor, Carlow College; Treasurer, Mr Michael Governey, C.U.D.C.; Secretary and Assistant Secretary, Michael O'Hanrahan and John Doyle. A Sub-Committee having been appointed to see after the working of the branch, the proceedings terminated. The class nights are Monday, Wednesday and Friday evenings at 8 o'clock. There is also a meeting on Sunday evenings, at which songs in Irish and English, readings, &c., are given. The subscriptions have been fixed at from 1/- to 5/- per year – Juveniles free.[3]

Thanks to his enthusiasm for the Irish language and his organisational precociousness, the years 1899 and 1900 brought Michael O'Hanrahan closer to Patrick Pearse and the leadership of the Gaelic League both physically and politically. Here, it is necessary to slightly amend the information in the *Dictionary of Irish Biography*, where the phrase (first formulated by Fr O'Flanagan in 1917 and much repeated since)[4] appears that Michael O'Hanrahan 'was a delegate of the Carlow branch to the second representative congress of the Gaelic League, held in Dublin in 1900'.[5] There is no need to doubt Michael's presence (which is recorded) at the national gathering of the Gaelic League in Dublin in 1900. But in fact it was a year earlier, in 1899, at what was the third Oireachtas of the Gaelic League that Michael first travelled up to Dublin to represent Carlow.

The first day of the 1899 Oireachtas, Wednesday 7 June, was largely taken up with the competitions in singing, recitation, oratory and dancing held in the Rotunda (for which admission was sixpence). And in the evening, with Cardinal Michael Logue, Primate of All Ireland, in the chair, various prizes were awarded. On the Thursday the more practical affairs of the Gaelic League were dealt with during a day-long meeting of the congress at the organisation's rooms at 24 Upper O'Connell Street. There, Michael O'Hanrahan spent the day as delegate from Carlow, speaking at least once (in favour of the next Oireachtas being held in Dublin as near as possible to the date of 1 May 1900).[6] In the evening a public meeting was held at the Mansion House, and here there was a real feeling that the movement for the resurrection of the Irish language was making headway.

As the report in the *Proceedings of the Third Oireachtas* put it: 'It may be said that the festivals of 1897 and 1898 were merely trials. Now, however, it was felt by all that the *Oireachtas* had become an institution, and that its influence for good in the fight for the language would be enormous.' And: 'On the conclusion of the proceedings it was felt that a remarkable advance on the road to success for the language movement had been made. Numbers of new adherents had been secured, while the workers felt encouraged to renewed exertion by the consciousness that the nation was at length commencing to realise the enormous importance of making one grand effort for the preservation of the native speech, without which a true Irish nation can never exist.'[7]

The *Proceedings* also noted the presence at this rally of the young man who had founded the Carlow branch of the Gaelic League. Among those listed as being either on the platform or in attendance was Michael O'Hanrahan.[8] There, too, were figures whose influence would be significant to O'Hanrahan: Eoin MacNeill, editor of the movement's new paper, *An Claidheamh Soluis*, and Patrick Pearse, who for the third Oireachtas acted as conductor of the competitions.

These were days of rapid growth for the Gaelic League: from having forty-three branches in 1897, it grew to eighty in 1899 and four hundred in 1902.[9] It might well have been that for some – including Michael O'Hanrahan – the language movement acted as a substitute for political organisation. The formal nationalist movement was still in the doldrums following its split from Parnell, and the revolutionary fragments of the IRB were yet to coalesce into a serious force. By contrast, the Gaelic League was proving itself. Firstly, in regard to the League's most urgent goal of reviving the Irish language, the 1901 census showed that while Irish usage had declined in the Gaeltacht, it had increased significantly elsewhere; in other words, as a result of people who had acquired Irish as a second language.[10] Secondly, those who joined and participated in Gaelic League activities were helping form a sense that within Ireland were cultural traditions that were quite distinct from, and more precious than, those of the British Empire. These included an authentic poetic tradition, worthy of world recognition; a legal corpus more sophisticated than that which existed in most regions of post-Roman Europe; an artistic culture with roots all the way back to Neolithic times; games and sports unknown to the Saxon world, and so forth. If some of the advocates of this revived Irish culture were prone to straining in a dewy-eyed and inventive fashion to build golden palaces out of mud bricks, theirs was an understandable reaction to the genuine danger that a precious historic culture was under threat of extinction.

One of the main demands of the Gaelic League was that

Irish be taught in schools, and the organisation's political lever for wresting this concession from Britain were the Urban District Councils and County Councils. The revived Carlow branch of the Gaelic League not only taught Irish but to some extent also acted as a political organisation, complete with teams of canvassers calling to houses in search of members.[11] By doing so, and as a result of raising demands upon candidates in the elections earlier in the year, the branch scored a heartfelt success at the meeting of Carlow County Council on Friday 12 May 1899, when the councillors passed the following resolution:

> That we, the Carlow County Council, respectfully urge on the educational authorities the great necessity of teaching the Irish Language in their establishments, and that we call on the Commissioners of National Education to introduce a system of bi-lingual education in the Irish-speaking districts. That copies of this resolution be sent to the Intermediate Commissioners and the Commissioners of National Education.[12]

Two months later, the Carlow Urban District Council and Board of Guardians passed a resolution in support of the Irish language, calling for bilingual teaching for the Irish-speaking districts. This was only the third Urban District Council to have done so.[13] That the Carlow branch did not just focus on teaching Irish was a source of criticism to some, and several years later, in 1906 – after Michael had moved to Dublin – it is possible to see an echo of this in a letter from 'Fear Eile' to *An Claidheamh Soluis* complaining that: 'In Ceatharloch, there is too little "language" and too much "movement"; the Craobh is in existence six or seven years and has never had an Irish class which went ten lessons beyond O'Growney II.'[14]

In addition to Michael's work in Carlow organising the Gaelic League branch, he also acted as a teacher of Irish for the classes at the Institute. From around this time onwards he adopted the Irish form of his name: Miceál Ua hAnnracáin (which I will henceforth use in this book). And it was under that name that he intervened in a growing rift between a nascent radical faction in the Gaelic League and *Fáinne an Lae*.

Because his was a commercial venture, Brian Ó Dubhghaill was a publisher and editor who was not fully responsible to the Gaelic League. At times, despite their admiration for his efforts, this created tension with the leaders of the Gaelic League, who were unhappy with the ambiguity of their relationship with the paper. For in the public eye, and indeed to members, *Fáinne an Lae* was very much seen as an official paper, well supplied in the minutes of Gaelic League meetings and copies of speeches. So when *Fáinne an Lae* took a view on a certain subject, it could easily be understood to be the view of the Gaelic League, even if, in fact, the League's executive saw matters differently. Wanting to have a more strictly aligned paper, the Gaelic League had launched *An Claidheamh Soluis* in March 1899, a paper under their direct control with Eoin MacNeill as editor.

For Miceál Ua hAnnracáin, this division obliged him to consider his loyalties. When he had first conceived of creating a branch of the Gaelic League in Carlow, *Fáinne an Lae* had been his inspiration. After the inaugural meeting in Carlow, Miceál had written to the paper, which he 'warmly commended for the exalted patriotism and unflinching courage that permeate every page of it'.[15] Now, however, he spoke out against the editor of *Fáinne an Lae*.

The opportunity to do so arose in the aftermath of the June 1899 congress in Dublin, to which, as noted above, Miceál Ua hAnnracáin was the Carlow delegate.[16] An anonymous column in *Fáinne an Lae* by 'X' claimed that a new constitution passed at the National Congress was leading to a dictatorship of the Dublin executive and Central Branch over the Gaelic League; that this harmed the idea of Irish self-government (by presenting a bad example); and that the limited number of members allowed onto the executive were too restrictive. In a letter of 15 July 1899, Miceál refuted the arguments of 'X' and concluded: 'The Central Branch has conducted the affairs of the League for the past six years in a manner highly creditable to themselves and the whole organisation … It is the Gaelic League that has made it possible for such papers as *Fáinne an Lae* to be carried on. And permit me to say that as the stated object of your paper is "the advancement of the Irish language", the remarks regarding the Central Council are very strange and entirely uncalled for.'[17]

With his letter generating hostile responses from 'X' and 'Sympathiser', and with 'X' accusing him of childishness, Miceál felt the need to write one further letter on the matter.

> I have interested myself sufficiently in Gaelic League matters as to be well acquainted with the facts which led up to the breach between the Gaelic League and *Fáinne an Lae* and even after these facts I do not think my confidence in the Gaelic League Executive is childish ... I admit the right of *Fáinne an Lae* or any other paper to criticise the action of societies like the Gaelic League, but I do not admit their right to criticise the Gaelic League in such a manner as *Fáinne an Lae* has done and is still doing.[18]

The final break with *Fáinne an Lae*, which was rapidly running out of funds now that there was an alternative Gaelic League paper, sheds some light on the emergence of a young militant faction of Gaelic League members, with whom Miceál Ua hAnnracáin can be numbered. While *Fáinne an Lae* was enthusiastic about Pan-Celtic activities and vigorously promoted the idea of an annual cultural festival in Ireland, Wales, Scotland, Cornwall, Brittany and the Isle of Man, *An Claidheamh Soluis* carried a ferocious attack on the project in its issue of 27 May 1899, seeing the consequent proposal to start a new Pan-Celtic movement with a headquarters in Dublin as a real threat to the success of the Gaelic League. Not only that, a purely cultural movement of Celts would fail to engage with the specifically Irish struggle against the British Empire that had attracted many of the League's members in the first place. An acting editor wrote in *An Claidheamh Soluis*:

It has been one of the misfortunes of Ireland that she ever looked to France or Spain or America rather than to the Galtees, to Cork, or to Donegal. The Gaelic League inculcates self-reliance and self-help. It teaches the Irish people that the future of the Irish language is in their own hands, that the language cannot be saved or destroyed by foreign influences. So far, this teaching has been successful. The Irish-speaking people are at last standing upon their feet, as they have not stood since the Treaty of Limerick. The Gaelic League has effected this revolution in thought, and there is no possible future development of the movement with which the League cannot keep pace. Why then should the League be displaced by a parasitic organisation, which seeks to divert to itself Irish energy and Irish money, and which cannot give in return any practical work, which teaches the old slavish doctrine of foreign dependence and which has been set in motion by a foreigner [a reference to Edmund Edward Fournier d'Albe, then teaching Maths at UCD] who cannot be expected to see the real needs of Ireland.[19]

Hitting back, a polemic by Brian Ó Dubhghaill exposed a faultline between the more politically focused Gaelic League organisers and figures like Hyde, whose emphasis was on culture. Indeed, the official editor of *An Claidheamh Soluis*, Eoin MacNeill, was sufficiently embarrassed by the 'self-reliance' editorial that he wrote a letter to a number of newspapers stating that the piece did not express the policy of the Gaelic League. Ó Dubhghaill was delighted.

When a man of Mr MacNeill's position in the movement is forced to send such a letter to the papers it is time something were done to curb the wild and, we might say, belligerent spirits who have control of the League publications – the youths of both sexes who imagine themselves the Heaven-sent leaders of the Language Revival, and who are thoroughly unfitted to take any prominent or responsible part in the conduct of a great National movement.[20]

And further:

Those wild and utterly incompetent individuals who are running the 'Organ' at the expense of the public should not be left in control of such a dangerous weapon as a newspaper, or any other publication in which they could have an opportunity of displaying their spleen or making abusive personal attacks.[21]

Wild, belligerent, dangerous. These were meant to be pejorative terms but to some they would have had quite the opposite appeal. The conflict was resolved soon after Patrick Pearse's attendance as delegate to the Welsh Eisteddfod later that year, with the following motion at the executive of the Gaelic League: 'This committee declares that, taken as a whole, the objects comprised under the title of Pan-Celticism extend beyond the scope of the Gaelic League. The Gaelic League, as a body, is therefore precluded from joining in a Pan-Celtic movement.'[22] Those in the Gaelic League who wanted a focus on matters Irish and, by implication, to intervene in policy issues concerning the language as well as in teaching and learning, were in a majority.

Chapter 4
• • • • •

1898–1901

The Workingman's Club

If Miceál Ua hAnnracáin's belief in the Irish language as a tool of emancipation made him part of an emerging group of young radicals within the Gaelic League, there was another field of interest that also attracted him, which was to help organise the workers of Carlow. Alongside Harry – as ever – Miceál enthusiastically assisted Tom Little (a letterpress machinist and Gaelic League supporter) in setting up a workingman's club for Carlow.

In England from the early 1860s, workingmen's clubs had flourished as places designed to cater for workers who wished to have a quiet space to read, play games, or relax that was not associated with the selling of alcohol. Such clubs were not to be confused with trade unions, whose creation often happened against very violent resistance from employers and the state; rather, they were looked at paternalistically by the elite, who saw them as an influence for social order.

One of the four objectives of the Club and Institute Union in Britain, for example, was 'to work for the reconciliation of classes. All classes could participate in the formation of clubs. Local gentlemen, by giving assistance and advice, would disabuse the working man of any notions that the interests of the classes were opposed.'[1]

In Ireland, while this same cross-class spirit was often present in the workingmen's clubs, another more radical one was there too. The Irish Republican Brotherhood found such clubs a useful place for holding discussions and finding recruits. So, for example, in 1891, police records show that the IRB had a presence in the Labour Leagues and Workingmen's Clubs of Kilkenny, Galway and Enniscorthy.[2]

In Carlow, the Workingman's Club was established by many of the same people who were involved in the Gaelic League, including the O'Hanrahan brothers. The minutes of this club survive back to its foundation and give considerable detail of Miceál's activities.[3] The idea of a workingman's club was first discussed in December 1898 in the home of Tom Little. 'Messrs. Little, O'Hanrahan, Ellis, Warren and McAssey were appointed to see Mr Molloy to enquire into the possibility of renting an early Georgian double house: No. 13, Brown St. Mr Molloy agreed to rent the premises for £7 a year and to be responsible for all structural repairs.'[4]

On 6 February 1899, Carlow's branch of the Typographical Association passed the following motion: 'We ... consider that the time has arrived when there should be established in this town a Trade's Council and Workman's Club, as we believe it would be for the protection of trade and labour, and safeguard the interests of all fair employers.'[5] This somewhat imprecise idea – there being a significant difference between a trades council and a club – took sharper form at a consequent meeting at the Town Hall on 11 February.

To that meeting, five members of every trade and five general labourers had been invited. Michael was one of those present, alongside his father Richard and brothers Edward and Harry.[6] There, John Murphy (Secretary of the Bakers Society) declined to act as chairman in favour of Tom Little, who then conducted the proceedings, making an opening speech outlining the advantages of such a club for the workers of Carlow. Because many trades were working on Saturdays, it was decided to have a follow-up meeting on a Sunday, to encourage a greater attendance. This took place on 26 February 1899, with Tom Little once more in the chair.

Letters in support of the establishment of a Carlow Workingman's Club were read from Bishop Patrick Foley and the IPP's John Hammond MP. There was to be a one-shilling entrance fee and – to allow any workingman to participate in the club – a figure of just two pence a week afterwards. The goal of the new club was primarily that of recreation for the workingmen of the town, outside of a pub environment. The men at the founding meeting proposed having a billiard table, a first-class reading room and different kinds of games, thus supplying 'a source of amusement, instruction, and interest'. Tom Little also made it clear that despite a rumour to the contrary, the club was not established on a political basis: 'They had not the remotest intention of doing any such thing, neither would they attempt to exclude any man on account of his political convictions.' Nor was the club in any way sectarian; whether Catholic or Protestant, the only criteria for membership would be that the applicant was a workingman.[7]

By this stage, the printers who had launched the idea of a club had clarified that although closely associated with the club, the Trades Council would be a different organisation. It was not, however, intended that the difference be that while the club was non-political, the Trades Council would play a more agitational role. During the course of his speech to the follow-up meeting of the Workingman's Club, Tom Little distanced himself from rumours that a Trades Council would be founded in order to challenge the employers of Carlow by demanding an eight-hour day and payment at ten pence per hour. 'They did not propose to move in that direction at all, nor did they propose to make it a lever for raising up the workingman against his employer. These were very far from being the real objects of the council.'[8]

The Trades Council would be composed of representatives from each trade and labour, and it would direct its operations to watching the interests of the trade and labour in Carlow. It would endeavour to keep work in the town, which was now done outside it, and by bringing pressure upon public men it would endeavour to have contracts for public institutions and such other matters carried out in Carlow. Sometimes they saw public contracts given away to strangers from other parts of Ireland who imported workmen, skilled and unskilled, from other places while the workmen of Carlow were left idle. The speaker explained the difference between Trades Council and a Trade and Labour Union. The principal point of difference which he dealt with was that the Trade and Labour Union devoted itself solely to the interests of the workers, while the Trades Council looked to the interests both of the employers and the employed in relation to competition from outside. In conclusion he appealed to the workingmen of Carlow to support to the utmost of their power the project whose details he had endeavoured to put before them.[9]

After discussion of Little's opening remarks, William Ellis (Secretary of the Typographical Association and also a Gaelic League member) proposed, 'that in the opinion of this meeting the proposal to establish a Workman's Club in Carlow deserves the hearty support of the town and neighbourhood; and the persons present pledge themselves to use their best exertions to make the undertaking successful'. This motion was seconded by electrician Michael Mulhall. A provisional committee was established and the Carlow Trades Council was formed.[10]

The first meeting of the Workingman's Club to be held at its new premises took place on Sunday 9 April 1899, with all three O'Hanrahan brothers present. There, Tom Little was elected President, while Harry O'Hanrahan became the Honorary Secretary. It is evidence of their high degree of organisational competence that despite being considerably younger than their peers in the Gaelic League and the Workingman's Club, the two O'Hanrahan brothers were both secretaries of these important new organisations for Carlow's artisans.

As secretary, on 8 July 1899 Harry wrote to Michael Governey, thanking him for a set of billiard table light shades that the factory owner had presented to the club. Governey, in turn, replied that it was 'a great pleasure to present the billiard light shades, as the advertisements on them will help to remind the members of the high-class and sparkling waters manufactured by Corcoran and Company Carlow'.[11]

Despite the avowed repudiation of politics, it did not take long for the Workingman's Club to become involved in local controversies and by doing so reveal that, regardless of Little's philosophy, the members were not following the socially conservative English model of a workingman's club. At a special meeting on Sunday 4 June 1899, the members intervened in a debate taking place at recent Urban District Council meetings by resolving to support a motion for the erection of artisans' dwellings, 'as we consider it a move in the right direction for the better housing of the working classes'. Another early resolution called on four committee members to wait on John Hammond MP and Michael Governey with a view to having more trade union representatives co-opted on the County Council. And in October 1899 it was agreed to send a letter to Carlow UDC protesting a decision to hold the election of Urban District Councillors every three years instead of annually. 'We feel,' stated the resolution, 'that this is meant to weaken the working man's influence on the Councillors.'[12]

A special meeting was held in June 1899 to pass three resolutions: one, to enforce sanitation laws by compelling local landlords to put their residential properties in order; two, to call upon Carlow UDC to support local industries by giving contracts to businessmen who employed local trade and labourers; and three, to call upon the UDC to see that all streets within the borough of Carlow be kept properly watered. Again, a willingness to challenge landlords emerged the following year: in May 1900, it was agreed that 'we, the members of Carlow Workman's club, protest against the injustice which is being perpetrated by certain local landlords by raising rents and we ask the Council to deter this act of tyranny'.[13]

A reflection of the interest of the members in politics is provided by the list of daily and weekly newspapers that were supplied to the club from newsagent Miss Colgan. Alongside titles providing entertainment – *Irish Bits, St Patrick's Strand, Harmsworth Harpers, Wide World, Chambers Irish Monthly, The Graphic, Black & White, Comic Cuts, Racing World, Golden Penny, Reynolds* and *Snapshots* – were those carrying local and international news. Some of these newspapers were of a broadly nationalist perspective – Carlow's *Nationalist and Leinster Times*, the *Irish Independent, Daily Freeman, The United Irishman, Leinster Leader* – but the club also ordered copies of the conservative and unionist newspapers: *The Irish Times, Carlow Sentinel* and *Herald Telegraph*. Irish literature was read in the form of the *New Ireland Review* and although the club was avowedly non-sectarian, it subscribed to the *Irish Catholic* and the *Irish Rosary*.

Miceál Ua hAnnracáin strove to shape the club so that as well as being representative of Carlow's skilled workers, it would be a force that supported the Irish language and nationalist ambitions. The Gaelic League's *An Claidheamh Soluis* was among the newspapers subscribed to at the club. At Miceál's motion, with the support of Little, a lamp was erected over the entrance with the name of the club in Irish: *Cumann na bhfear oibre Cheatharlach*. Within two months of the formation of the club, the following resolution was passed: 'We, the members of Carlow Workman's Club, pledge ourselves by every means in our power to forward the interest of the Gaelic League, Ceatharlach.' A further resolution by Miceál, proposed 12 February 1900 and carried unanimously, was that:

1. In places where Irish is the home language, pupils should be taught to read and write in Irish from their first day in school.

2. Where Irish is not the home language it shall be lawful to teach Irish as a remunerative subject during school hours at the earliest possible stage at which pupils are capable of learning it.

3. Copies of this resolution to be sent to the Chief Secretary of the Commissioners for National Education, the whips of the Irish Party, the members in this division, the metropolitan press and the Secretary of the Gaelic League.[14]

Also in 1900, Miceál Ua hAnnracáin successfully proposed that a Workingman's Club parade would be held every November to 'Croppy Graves' in Graigue as part of a Manchester Martyrs Commemoration. Local and outside bands would be hired. This was a major departure from the 'non-political' type of club that had provided the model for the Carlow initiative. But no doubt it was a decision that was in keeping with the outlook of the town at the time, and especially those thousands who had marched for the 1798 commemorations. Again, a nationalist sentiment among the club's committee was evident in 1900 when they learned that the Protestant church in the Carlow Asylum was buying its furniture from England. Miceál Ua hAnnracáin put a resolution to the committee that they contact the church with the following message: 'We respectfully urge upon you the necessity of giving this contract to an Irish firm. The workmanship of Irish tradesmen, although perhaps more costly, is superior to English and Scottish produces.' Passed unanimously, copies of the resolution were sent to the management of Carlow Asylum and Dublin Trades Council.[15]

There was, however, a tension within the committee between radical young members like the O'Hanrahan brothers Harry and Miceál, and those of a more conservative, Redmondite persuasion. Within two months of the club having been founded, Harry resigned as Honorary Secretary, stating 'that owing to some members of the club marking complaints against himself and his brother he had determined to resign his position'. Chairman Tom Little, wanting to keep the O'Hanrahans in the club, impressed upon Harry the necessity of retaining his position and asked him as a favour to reconsider his decision. Harry did so a few days later, announcing that he had reconsidered his determination of resigning and would continue to hold office.[16]

The club committee was divided, too, over the intervention of Miceál and Harry at a pro-British series of film

screenings, designed to raise funds for those who had suffered as a result of the fighting in the Boer War. The report of
the incident in *The Nationalist and Leinster Times* in January
1900 ran under the heading 'War Concert in Carlow':

Head Constable McCoy, whose talent for organising public
entertainment has long been recognised, has been devoting
his efforts to the aid of the various funds for the relief of the
sufferers by the war. He has got up three grand concerts,
varied by limelight views of the scenes from South Africa.

The first concerts were on Monday (mid-day) and night,
they were well attended.

The seeds of future disorder were sown when some ultra
Britishers hissed President Kruger's effigy as shown on the
screen. Later further irritation was caused by the singing
of 'God Save The Queen', a tune which has unfortunately
been made a party one in Ireland.

On Tuesday night every picture of the Boers was cheered
whilst the British generals and in fact every scene favour-
able to the British was hissed vigorously. The picture of the
disaster to a British armoured train was loudly cheered. At
the end 'The Boys of Wexford' was sung by the vast majority of the audience, the strains of the Royal anthem being
completely drowned.

Any reference of a pro-British tendency called for marked
disapproval.

> A voice from the back was heard, 'Well done, young blood of Carlow'.
>
> ... the Head Constable engaged in a wordy contest with the 'voice' at the back and offered to bet £10 that the 'voice' would not name a freer country than Ireland.
>
> On Thursday night suspected Boer sympathisers were excluded, but the 'Boers' invaded and turned out the gas and left the whole place in darkness.
>
> The entertainments raised over £40. The Hall was decorated by Misses Duggan, Burke, Langran, Hearns.
>
> The Union Jack we may say was the prevailing ornament.

This victory for the 'Boers' over Head Constable McCoy and the ultra-Britishers was co-ordinated by the O'Hanrahans, and as the tone of the *Nationalist* indicates, it was not a victory about which the Irish Party were particularly enthusiastic. A month after the disruption of the film, Henry McAteer of the Irish Transvaal Committee arrived in Carlow with clandestine leaflets aimed at discouraging recruitment to the British Army; the IRB was the key organisation for their distribution. It is highly likely, given Miceál and Harry's leadership of the pro-Boer protests and Richard O'Hanrahan's old contacts with the IRB, that McAteer met Miceál Ua hAnnracáin, but this has to be guesswork given the secretive nature of IRB activity.[17]

The division between moderate and radical nationalists in regard to the Boer War flared up again at the Workingman's

Club when a British officer applied to join as a member, and this time it brought about the resignation of the O'Hanrahan brothers. In 1881, the Carlow Militia had been reorganised into the 'foreign legion' that was the King's Royal Rifle Corps and that regiment had fought at the Battle of Talana Hill in the Boer War on 20 October 1899. In February 1901, J Hopkins, a member of staff of 8th Battalion, KRR, applied for admission to the club. This was a real test of the committee and from Harry and Miceál's point of view the decision was a crucial one. Once British soldiers were allowed into the club, it would immediately be less safe for advocates of radical nationalism. At first, a decision on whether to allow the British officer to be a member was deferred, 'as some members of the committee stated that this person had applied before for admission and he was rejected on account of his belonging to the army'.[18]

Chairman Little informed a meeting of the committee on 11 February 1901 that the minute book had been searched for the information required, but no minute related to the case could be found. It was therefore the duty of the committee to go into the matter and see if Hopkins was eligible for membership. Miceál Ua hAnnracáin then proposed and J Kelly seconded a resolution to the effect that the soldier not be admitted as a member. A very long discussion ensued on the proposition. In favour of admitting Hopkins were Michael Mulhall, as proposer, and John Brennan, as seconder.

The debate on the proposition and amendment continued for so long that members of the committee suggested the matter be adjourned in order to subsequently convene a special meeting of the committee.

At that further meeting, on 19 February 1901, the discussion resumed for some time. During the course of the heated debate, Miceál Ua hAnnracáin informed the meeting that in the event of Hopkins being admitted as a member, he would resign his seat on the committee and terminate his membership of the club. Ultimately a vote was taken, which resulted as follows: For the amendment: six, including John Brennan. Against: four; Harry and Miceál as well as P and J Kelly. The Chairman, Tom Little, abstained. The amendment was declared carried. Miceál therefore promptly tendered his resignation and after listening to some complimentary remarks from the Chairman on his contribution to the founding of the club, left the meeting. The remaining committee members, including Harry, resolved to write to Miceál Ua hAnnracáin to ask him to reconsider his decision.

There was no political difference in outlook between Harry and Miceál, and no doubt Harry would have walked out after the vote on 19 February too, were it not for his responsibilities as Honarary Secretary. But within a month, he too had resigned, stating 'that as soldiers had been elected members of the club he would resign his membership as a protest'.[19]

Chairman Tom Little was anxious to rebuild bridges to the O'Hanrahan brothers, but not all the remaining members of the committee felt the same way. In particular, the same members who had led the argument in favour of the entry of Hopkins to the club – Brennan and Mulhall – now demonstrated how bitter the breach had become when they called a special committee meeting on Thursday 14 March 1901, just six days after Harry's resignation, to threaten legal action against him over his possession of a cue belonging to the club.

At the committee meeting a fortnight later, letters were read from Miceál Ua hAnnracáin, Harry and fellow resignee John Donnelly (an agent for the Phoenix Brewing Company) outlining their reasons for resigning from the club and answering the allegations with regard to the missing cue.

From 1898 to 1902, Miceál and Harry had emerged as leading organisers of those of a radical nationalist persuasion in Carlow by orientating towards their peers among artisans and the skilled working class and by putting in hard work for the Gaelic League, the 1798 commemorations, and the Workingman's Club. Miceál, in particular, from the age of twenty-one was out nearly every night of the week to attend the meetings and events of one organisation or another, or at GAA training. Through such intense effort, harnessed to organisations that were unmistakably on the rise, Miceál was embarking on a course that would see him play a central role in Ireland's history. In other words, by eschewing the existing conservative nationalist organisations and helping create – from nothing – the Gaelic League and the Workingman's Club in Carlow, he had found a path that allowed for the rapid advance of the struggle for Irish independence. His actions as a young man were prescient for the nation, but fateful for him personally.

There was nothing in the manner of the man that Miceál had become in his early twenties to suggest that the drive behind his organising work arose from a desire to view himself in the mirror as a national hero. The dedication with which Miceál pursued his goals was combined with a modest, thoughtful demeanour. As Eily put it: 'I am his sister and, therefore, perhaps should not say it, Micheál had an unusually nice character. He was gentle, quiet and unassuming. He was devoted to his home and loved home life, although he was so active in the Gaelic League movement and the Volunteers that he spent a lot of his time away from home.'[20]

Similar testimony of this character was given to the *The Kerryman* on the fiftieth anniversary of the Rising. 'His convictions were as steady as a rock. They appeared to have been part of the man's mental and spiritual make-up. Outwardly, he did not suggest any of the qualities which are usually, and often mistakenly, associated with leadership. The glow of the inward fire was felt only by those who were privileged to have intimate relations with him.'[21] Again, this outward calm and inward passion caught the attention of Fr O'Flanagan: 'Michael O hAnnrachain was one of those modest, silent, earnest workers who do not seek applause, and who are only revealed to the public in the flare of a great crisis. The gold of human character does not always glitter. It is often effectively hidden behind a modest and unassuming exterior.'[22]

Kitty O'Doherty, quartermaster of Cumann na mBan, who later lived on the same street as the O'Hanrahans in Dublin, also remembered Miceál as quiet and retiring.[23] TD Sinnott recalled that, 'As Quartermaster his principal concern was with arms and ammunition and many of us here present can still recall his quiet, unassuming and terribly earnest handling of munitions and arms – questions at a time when money was as scarce amongst us as modern weapons of offence.'[24] And a further confirmation that Eily was not simply expressing a sisterly bias comes from an unusual source, with the Dublin detective Halley describing Miceál and Harry as 'two quiet inoffensive men'.[25] Quiet and inoffensive personally, but Miceál was on a course to become very dangerous to British authority in his untiring efforts to organise radical nationalists on a number of fronts.

Chapter 5

• • • • •

1902–1909

The National Organiser

For some years, Miceál and Harry had been travelling to Dublin to participate in various nationalist organisations, most especially the Gaelic League. Harry C Phibbs, a member of the Celtic Literary Society before his emigration to America, recalled meeting the two brothers in Walker's tobacco shop on High Street, while they were still residents of Carlow. Walker's had a small hall at the back at which many of those interested in the Irish language would meet, including Sinéad Ní Fhlannagáin (Éamon de Valera's future wife), Michael Mallin, later second-in-command of the Citizen Army, IRB activists Liam Mellows and Seán MacDiarmada, and Sean Barlow, stage manager of the Abbey Theatre.[1] Walker, who owned the premises, was well known to the O'Hanrahan brothers as he was from Carlow, where he had owned a small Parnellite newspaper and had been effectively ruined by the success of his Irish Party rivals.[2]

As a result of declining business in Carlow, the O'Hanrahan family took a decision to move to Dublin. With the exception of Edward – who had just married and was happy in Carlow with his job in the Postal Service – the O'Hanrahans (Mary and Richard, along with Harry, Miceál, Eily, Anna and Máire) relocated to the capital. There, they attempted to set up a corkcutting business in a small premises south of the river near the Bank of Ireland.[3] With the premature death of Richard, however, soon after the move, the family gave up corkcutting and found the premises for a shop and family rooms at 67 Connaught Street in Phibsboro. Having set up a tobacco and fancy goods store, Anna and Máire ran the shop, Eily went to study art, while Miceál and Harry looked for work. Later, Máire found employment at 12s. 6d. a week which she regarded as 'a very small wage' but given the difficult family circumstances, she felt that this was a useful contribution to the household income.[4]

That the death of Richard was a very heavy blow to the family and that their mother Mary helped pull them through the crisis is indicated by Miceál's dedication to his 1914 novel, *A Swordsman of the Brigade*. There, he wrote, 'To the memory of a father to whom I owe much, whose life's quest is over, and to one other, my mother, who whispered hope when days were black, I dedicate this book.'

For several years, Harry – with help from Miceál and probably a certain amount of knowledge gleaned from their uncle Watty O'Hanrahan's business experience – tried his hand at printing bill-posters, street advertisements, tickets, etc. He founded a small shop at 144 Capel Street with the name of The Express Advertising Co.[5] For Miceál, however, his main desire was to find a job that would allow him to keep up as high a level of involvement in the national movement as possible, a desire which led him to become proofreader of the Cló Cumann Printing Company on Strand Street, central Dublin. Cló Cumann was the printing office set up by a number of Gaelic Leaguers to help produce nationalist books, particularly those written in Gaelic, and they needed a proofreader skilled in Irish. It seems likely that the IRB had considerable influence over appointments to Cló Cumann, as from 1905 the manager of the company was PT Daly, who was also a leading figure in Dublin's IRB. Having served his apprenticeship as a printer, Daly was also a councillor at the time, representative of the Rotunda Ward seat on Dublin's corporation for the National Council, elected in September 1903.

In 1908, socialist thinker and activist James Connolly vouched for Daly in the most glowing terms when writing for American readers on news from Ireland:

I know PT Daly personally. He is a young man, a compositor by trade, and with an absolutely clean record. His first participation in public life was as a speaker at meetings in connection with the Old Guard Benevolent Union, an organization of veterans of the Fenian movement, and of those who subscribed to the principles of that movement.

Most of the members of this body were earnest whole-souled enthusiasts, but quite a few, especially those who joined during the Centenary Celebrations of the Rebellion of 1798, were wire-pullers who desired to use the Old Guard for personal purposes. I have always classed Daly among the former number.

Fortunately for him he had read most of the literature sold by the Irish Socialist Republican Party, and all of the literature published under the authority of, and by that body. In fact as a compositor he had helped to set it up, as it was printed to a great extent in the shop where he was employed. Such reading helped, no doubt, to steady him at a time when much foolish matter about the 'union of classes' was being preached in Ireland.

Since then he has become a Sinn Féiner, been elected to the Dublin City Council, and has always, so far as we know, lined up on the right side.[6]

Police reports indicate that there were just fifty-six active members of the IRB in Dublin in 1902, with about as many again nominal members.[7] But soon to become chief among them was PT Daly. The records of police informers show Daly working nationally for the IRB from 1902 and he reputedly became president of the Supreme Council in 1907.[8] In all likelihood, Daly's working companion in the Strand Street print-shop, Miceál Ua hAnnracáin, was a fellow IRB member at the time he was recuited to the job. Miceál might well have been one of the sixty republicans that the police claimed existed in the town of Carlow in the early 1900s: after all, it was IRB policy to favour the Redmondites in the 1798 commemorations; to attempt to recruit from within workingman's clubs; to be involved in the GAA; to support the Boers in their war against the Empire; and of course Miceál's father was an old IRB member.[9] If so, then it might well have been the good word from IRB contacts – as well, of course, as his mastery of Irish – that assisted Miceál in finding work at Cló Cumann.

According to Proinnsias Ó Dubhthaigh, National Council member and Captain of 'C' Company of the Enniskillen Battalion of the Volunteers, Miceál Ua hAnnracáin never joined the IRB. 'I discussed the question of the IRB and the Volunteers, in July 1915, with Michael O'Hanrahan … who was then on the staff of the Volunteer headquarters office, and whom I had known intimately for many years. He was aware of the fact that many of the higher Volunteer officers were members of the IRB, but he had refused to join that organisation, and he was strongly of the opinion that its existence in the Volunteers was unnecessary and might lead to confusion.' As a result of being impressed by this argument, said Ó Dubhthaigh, he let his own IRB membership lapse.[10]

Ó Dubhthaigh had come to advanced nationalist politics through the Carlow branch of the Gaelic League that Miceál had founded and, indeed, was secretary of the branch soon after Miceál's departure. So there are good grounds for accepting that he knew Miceál well enough to receive this candid testimony. Yet on the other hand, Ó Dubhthaigh was actively hostile to the IRB in his time as a Volunteer officer in Monaghan. It is quite likely, in fact, that Miceál was already an IRB member at the time of this conversation and that in order to avoid difficulties at headquarters with non-IRB figures like Eoin MacNeill and The O'Rahilly, Miceál deceived Ó Dubhthaigh on the issue of his IRB membership.

That Miceál did join the IRB at some point was stated by a well-informed piece about him in the *Carlow Nationalist* in June 1920 and by his sister Eily to the *New Ross Standard* in 1948. Eily herself was a member of the Wolfe Tone Memorial Committee, North Ward, a cover organisation for the IRB, which included among its members IRB veteran Tom Clarke. In her 1948 interview, Eily stated that 'he [Miceál] was the intimate and trusted friend of Pearse, Clarke and McDermott and was constantly in conference with the Supreme Council of the IRB.'[11] According to Frank Henderson, Harry, too, worked for the IRB for years before the Rising and 'almost certainly carried out orders of the IRB Military Council'. Indeed, 'all members of his family including himself were devoted members of the revolutionary organisation and worked for it for long years unobtrusively'.[12]

That Miceál was an IRB member in 1910 is implied by the fact that as 'Art', he prepared a short piece on the Fianna for the launch of the IRB's monthly newspaper, *Irish Freedom*, in November 1910. Given the IRB's persistent attempt to recruit all the senior Volunteers that they could, and given also the close attention paid by the IRB to the question of control over finances and the arms of the Volunteers, Miceál could hardly have played the role he did without being an IRB member.[13] As will be seen, Miceál did become Quartermaster General for the Rising and knew of the timing of the insurrection as soon as the Military Council of the IRB had agreed upon it.

Having settled in Dublin, Miceál immediately found himself a role in the Dublin nationalist movement, naturally as an active Gaelic League member and GAA member – he and Harry joined the St Laurence O'Toole GAC[14] – but also in an organisation that sprang up in response to an impending royal visit to Ireland. In the summer of 1902, a regrouping of Dublin nationalists took place to make sure that the planned 1903 visit of Edward VII was met with major protests. When the royal parade came to Dublin on 21 July 1903, the protesters, although a minority of those watching, were vocal enough that their cries of opposition were very noticeable.[15] One lasting gain for the nationalist movement from this campaign was the formation of a new organisation, An Chomhairle Náisiúnta, or the National Council, not least thanks to the efforts of Arthur Griffith, a newspaper editor recently returned from South Africa. The National Council, with offices at 6 Harcourt Street, functioned as a vehicle to unite nationalists who found the IPP too moderate, and among its leading members was PT Daly.

An Chomhairle Náisiúnta came to prominence in 1906, with the Irish Party (IPP) losing their influence in Westminster as a result of the elections that year. Suddenly, alternatives to the IPP's strategy for obtaining Home Rule were being sought by those who up to then had taken for granted that there would soon be some kind of devolution of power to a Dublin parliament. An Chomhairle Náisiúnta began to grow, establishing branches in Belfast, Cork, Kilkenny, Waterford and Cavan; additionally, individuals wrote in from all over the country seeking to join. Needing a full-time organiser, Griffith and the other officers of the organisation asked for the assistance of Miceál Ua hAnnracáin.

A membership card (belonging to County Donegal republican activist Denis Phelan) for the National Council dated 1906 confirms that Miceál had a leading role in that body in that year, for it shows the signature of the playwright Edward Martyn as President and underneath, 'M. Ua hAnnracháin'.[16] Again, a letter to Liam de Roiste – later a Volunteer and a TD – on An Chomhairle Náisiúnta notepaper is

signed by Miceál in 1906.[17] While organising for An Chomhairle Náisiúnta, Miceál Ua hAnnracáin represented the
organisation at a meeting in January 1906 to support radical
nationalist John Kelly in the Inns Quay ward for an election to Dublin Corporation.[18] In the Mountjoy ward for the
same elections, Miceál helped put National Council support
behind James Gaffney, who was a supporter of the labour
movement as well as of advanced nationalism. Gaffney was
a member of No. 3 Branch Carpenters Society and had also
the support of the Dublin United Trades Council.[19]

That Miceál had the right qualities for the role of organiser for An Chomhairle Náisiúnta had become evident over
the previous year. During 1905, Norway had given nationalists another example of the possibility of the escape of one
country from the monarchy of another when, on 7 June
1905, the Norwegian parliament declared its separation from
the Swedish Crown. In a referendum in August, 99.95 percent of the Norwegian population voted to end the union.
Although there was resistance to these political developments
by Sweden, on 26 October 1905 King Oscar II of Sweden
renounced his claim to the Norwegian throne and the Nor-
wegians celebrated their newly acquired independence. In
Ireland, a meeting was held in solidarity with Norway at the
Rotunda, and Miceál Ua hAnnracáin was the secretary for
the event.[20]

Briefly co-existing with An Chomhairle Náisiúnta was

Cumann na nGaedheal, an organisation inspired by the writings of Arthur Griffith that had existed since 1900, and the Dungannon Clubs, a 1905 initiative of the Belfast-based IRB organiser John Bulmer Hobson, who had particular success in establishing these clubs in Northern Ireland. Having demonstrated the possibility of successfully outflanking the established nationalist parties, Hobson then came to Dublin in 1907 and helped create the Sinn Féin League under the presidency of PT Daly by merging the Dungannon Clubs with Cumann na nGaedheal. One of the first meetings of the Sinn Féin League was on the topic of Irish industry in the light of a major exhibition being planned for Dublin by British manufacturers. At that meeting, 'the discussion was ably sustained by Mr O'Hanrahan'. It is interesting to note that Miceál followed Daly in supporting the Sinn Féin League, and this also strongly suggests he was an IRB member at the time.[21]

After some complex manoueverings, Arthur Griffith accepted the merger of An Chomhairle Náisiúnta with the Sinn Féin League to form a new political movement, Sinn Féin, in 1907. Two years previously, Griffith – briefly an IRB member until this new initiative – had launched the Sinn Féin Policy with a three-hour lecture at a National Council meeting at the Rotunda Club on 28 November 1905.[22] This was a relatively small meeting at which Miceál Ua hAnnracáin was present alongside Patrick Pearse and Patrick McCartan.

The historical significance of the moment was not evident to the participants, and a sense of the anti-climatic atmosphere of that launch meeting is contained in the memoirs of Cahir Healy, poet and Fermanagh delegate to the event:

> Griffith's written speech read much better in his paper the week after than it did that day. Seumas MacManus and PS O'Hegarty talked a good deal ... Griffith had just published serially his 'Resurrection of Hungary' and everyone pretended to see the parallel [with Ireland]. It was all over in a little while, and when we came into the street and mingled with the crowd, it seemed to me very much like the river that rushes to the ocean, to be instantly engulfed therein. The press took no notice.[23]

The pamphlet referred to, 'The Resurrection of Hungary', which was first published in 1904, had sold an astonishing 30,000 copies by February 1905 and went on to sell over 300,000 copies by the Easter Rising. In many ways, such as in its acceptance of the principle of monarchy, Griffith's work was not particularly radical. But the appeal of the pamphlet and of Griffith's nascent party was that it demonstrated that countries which had once been governed by the same political structures and bureaucracy could separate out into two distinct entities. This idea contrasted with the philosophy of John Redmond and the reunited Irish Party, for whom autonomy for Ireland never went beyond the goal of

having 'Home Rule': an Irish parliament within the Empire.
Despite the popularity of Griffith's writings, Sinn Féin was
slow to make progress and the IRB ordered a number of
Dublin members to augment the meagre attendances of the
party at its Harcourt Street offices.[24] Having come to Sinn
Féin – via both An Chomhairle Náisiúnta and the Sinn Féin
League – Miceál now had yet another organisation to which
he gave his time and energy.

In the course of his efforts to develop Sinn Féin, Miceál
travelled to Newry on Saturday 17 August 1907 to address
an open rally on behalf of the new organisation. At 8.30pm,
Miceál and the other speakers arrived in a brake (a form of
horse-drawn carriage) at Margaret Square, where the rally
was due to begin. Unfortunately, loyalists from as far afield
as Belfast had mobilised to ensure the meeting was a failure (as had supporters of the United Irish League, a rival
to the IPP that saw the development of Sinn Féin as a serious threat to their aspiration of achieving hegemony of the
national movement). The hostility of the 2,000-strong crowd
awaiting the vehicle was extremely intimidating. Stones were
thrown, injuring one of the other speakers and a journalist.
Having retained his calm and addressed the crowd as well
as he could, Miceál turned around and was surprised by
the fact that he stood alone on the brake. The other speakers – including Bulmer Hobson and his Dungannon Club
co-founder Denis McCullough – had fled. Miceál got away

unharmed when the brake was driven away, followed by the jeering crowd.[25]

Thanks to his work for Arthur Griffith, Miceál Ua hAnnracáin was able to develop his skills as a writer, for Griffith had established the newspaper *Sinn Féin*, to which Miceál contributed an article each week under the pseudonym of 'Art'. In these, Miceál wrote with humour – no easy feat – on the political affairs of interest to nationalists. Generally, the columns took the form of a dialogue between Johnny and Martin, two imaginary wags who enjoyed picking over the news of the day or some phrase or other uttered by a public figure. One early appraisal of these columns, written in 1917, analysed them as showing 'a steady improvement in style and construction', which indicated that 'the young writer had a bright future before him'.[26] The political thought that inspired Miceál and underlay his satirical journalism derived from the writings of 1803 insurrectionary Robert Emmet, the Young Irelander James Fintan Lalor, and John Mitchel, author of the famous *Jail Journal* (1854).[27]

From Miceál's writings, it becomes clear that this quiet and unassuming figure, who worked behind the scenes as much as possible, was passionately convinced that only armed rebellion would separate Ireland from the Empire. For example, in the first issue of *Irish Freedom* in 1910 he wrote, 'The history of the world proves that there is but one road to freedom, and that is the red road of war. The editorial, the article, or the speech, however eloquent, which does not point out that road is so much cant which only further enslaves an enslaved people from the fact that it urges on them the false path which leads to confusion and demoralization … We have set ourselves to the task of preparing both mentally and physically for the great day, on the eve of which those of us who have survived will see, with gladsome eyes, Cathleen Ni Houlihan launch Fair Freedom's ship with the Republican colours at the mast in the blood of the Saxon.'[28]

It is also evident that Miceál was reading very widely, following closely the political affairs of the day and even obtaining newspapers from France and Switzerland to find information about events in Egypt and India that were not being reported in the British press.[29] From such information he wrote columns not only urging Irish solidarity with those countries, but also that the people of India and Egypt should themselves prepare to 'drive the British enemy from their land'.[30]

It was in Miceál's work for the Gaelic League, as much as in his writings, that he really began to emerge as a nationally recognised figure. On 25 May 1904, at the annual meeting of the Ard Craobh of the Gaelic League, both Miceál and Harry were nominated for the executive committee that ran the League, with Miceál being elected.[31] In 1905, he was also elected to the committee to establish Coláiste Múinteoireachta Laighean, the Leinster College of Irish. This college opened on 1 October 1906, holding evening classes in Dublin on Mondays and Thursdays and with future Rising leader Éamonn Ceannt as registrar.[32]

On 20 August 1905, several Dublin cultural nationalist organisations arranged for an excursion to the Hill of Tara and a rally there at the end of the Gaelic League's Oireachtas. The event took place on a beautiful Sunday, with the hill warmed by bright sunshine. The veteran nationalist organiser Jennie Wyse Power brought a large marquee for the catering.[33] Wyse Power had been involved in the Ladies' Land League and was a founder member of both Inghinidhe na hÉireann (Daughters of Ireland), a nationalist women's organisation, and Sinn Féin. Thousands attended and enjoyed the songs, dances and instrumental music.

The organiser of the event and the person with responsibility for the finances of the day was Miceál Ua hAnnracáin. Because he and Harry had to settle the accounts in connection with the trip, they, along with Wyse Power and her son, aged twelve, missed the return train to Dublin. The two brothers went to Coady's pub in Tara to obtain a room for the night but were refused because the proprietor, Elizabeth Coady, was a staunch loyalist who did not approve of the day's events. The door was slammed in their faces, and Elizabeth Coady refused to arrange a car for the small party. Nor would the stationmaster let them spend the night in the station. On the roadside late at night, a stranger took pity on them and persuaded Elizabeth Coady to let Jennie Wyse Power and her son spend the night at the pub. Miceál and Harry got a lift as far as Dunshaughlin, after which they walked through the night, arriving home at 5am on the Monday.

Although they were unable to challenge the hotel owner at the time, the O'Hanrahan brothers did not let the matter rest and took a suit against the hotel. It was the defence of the owner that Miceál and Harry were 'persons of no means and no consequence'.[34] The suit came to the Trim Quarter Sessions before County Court Judge Adye Curran: 'O'Hanrahan vs Mrs Elizabeth Coady of Kilmessan'. Miceál was claiming damages for her breach of duty as an innkeeper, but he lost his case when the judge adjudicated that although an innkeeper would have been liable, the Coadys' licence for a public house did not necessarily make them innkeepers. This decision was made despite the fact that there was no distinction between hotel and publican licenses in the country districts at the time and it was demonstrated that there was no one else staying at the house on the night. Under cross-examination, Elizabeth Coady denied her premises were a hotel, even though it was also pointed out to her that the billheads of the premises read 'Wingfield Arms Hotel'. Coady also kept a visitor's book which contained, among other names of guests, those of the Duke and Duchess of Westminster, and, indeed, that of … Judge Adye Curran. There was no shaming Judge Curran into acknowledging the justice of the case taken by the O'Hanrahan brothers, and he threw it out.[35]

That by this stage of his life Miceál was seen as utterly reliable when it came to the handling of public money was shown again in 1908. In September that year a boat with a crew of nineteen sailors from Portmagee was overturned near Valentia Island in the dead of night in a strong ebb tide. Thirteen of the men were rescued, but six others drowned. Miceál Ua hAnnracáin was made treasurer of a Dublin Collection Committee to raise money for the families of the dead, which was able to forward a substantial cheque – over £350 – in December 1908. Miceál moved a vote of thanks from the committee to the Keating Branch of the Gaelic League, who allowed the organisation to use its rooms.[36] The transparency of the finances of this collection was evident in that all donations to it, large or small, were acknowledged in the press.[37]

In 1905, Miceál became secretary of the Ard Craobh of the Gaelic League, and was a member of the Dublin district committee. The following year he was on the subcommittee of the Gaelic League for the organisation of the annual *feis*. This meant giving up alternate Saturday nights for those meetings.[38] By 1908, he – alongside Pádraic Mac Giolla Iosa (Pat Ingoldsby) – was a key figure in the organisation of the annual language procession in Dublin, being an active member of the language week committee. In 1909, Miceál was secretary of this language procession committee.

Launched by the Gaelic League, language processions were enormous public demonstrations of support for Ireland's language and past culture. The first of these took place on 16 March 1902, and as it took about three hours to pass a given point, the march must have been some 100,000 strong. The parade ended with a monster meeting in Smithfield. Up until this time, St Patrick's Day was an ordinary working day, but one of the goals of the procession was to make it a holiday, and placards raising this demand were eagerly taken up.[39]

The creation of an official holiday on St Patrick's Day became law in 1903 with the passage in February of the Bank Holidays (Ireland) Bill. On the motion of the IPP, the Bill sanctioned a development that had been occurring in any case, that of a widely observed holiday, one which was, as the Earl of Dunraven put it in the Commons debates, 'universally desired by all classes in Ireland'.[40] Dunraven's statement wasn't entirely correct, as according to Seamus Ua Caomhanaigh (a future member of the Sinn Féin Executive), it 'took a lot of argument and a lot of hard work' to get business owners to sign a pledge to close their establishments.[41] Publicans only fell in line with the passing of the Bill.

With the Gaelic League's procession now a firmly established tradition and associated with a legal bank holiday, the celebrations of 1904 should have been huge, but they were destroyed by weather described in the *Irish Independent* and in

Eamonn Ceannt's private notes on the event as 'rain, pitiless rain'. The *Irish Independent* added that the rain came down in torrents at one o'clock, when the crowds were assembling literally in their thousands.[42]

The procession of 12 March 1905 saw two forms of protest. The first was the unofficial expulsion of a horse-drawn carriage holding DP Moran, editor and owner of *The Leader*. This occurred – by a daring young man, wearing an armband as though an official, taking the horse's head and leading the carriage away – because the paper had been vilifying the Coiste Gnótha (executive committee) of the Gaelic League by insinuating that the money collected at the parade was being misspent. 'These charges,' Seamus Ua Caomhanaigh told the Military Bureau much later, 'repeated week after week on the eve of the collection exasperated all those hard-working Gaelic Leaguers who were spending day and night working without rest to ensure the success of the objects of the League.'[43] A furious Moran later attempted to mobilise his supporters within the Gaelic League to obtain a humbling apology from the Coiste Gnótha, but failed in this effort.[44] Secondly, an official and powerful protest against the anti-Irish attitude of the GPO was expressed dramatically in striking tableau repeated in hundreds of printed legends.

An organising letter dated 13 February 1906, from the Gaelic League's offices of 24 Upper O'Connell Street, was drafted by the committee at a meeting attended by Harry. The letter announced a 'Demonstration to inaugurate Irish Language Week' and invited 'Branches of the Gaelic League, the various Trades' Societies, Schools, Colleges, Temperance Associations, Clubs, Bands and other Bodies and Organisations' to send two delegates to City Hall later in the month, from which assembly the plan of the march was adopted.[45]

For the 1907 parade, which was held in June, the Tableaux Committee drew up a list of scenes from Ireland's past and the branches were invited to stage representations of these moments. The eight tableaux were drawn from a curious mix of fable and history: the mythological period; the Cuchulainn Cycle; tales of Oisín and Niamh; tales of Oisín and Patrick; the Viking era; the Norman era; the O'Neill and O'Donnell period and the Confederation of Kilkenny period. The mass meeting was in Smithfield that year, with Douglas Hyde giving the main address.

It was in regard to the 1908 Irish Language Week that Miceál Ua hAnnracáin came forward as one of the main organisers of these massive events. Indeed, in the eyes of the authorities Miceál was the parade's main representative, as he was the person who applied to the Board of Works for permission to use Phoenix Park on Sunday 20 September for the event. Because of the danger of poor weather, a decision had been made to move the language procession first to June and then, because of concerns that numbers would

Above: Michael O'Hanrahan was born in New Ross in 1877, where his father Richard had a corkcutting business.

Below: The family later moved to Carlow and set up a house, shop and workshop at 90 and 91 Tullow Street.

Left: This photograph of sixty women who had been involved in the Rising was taken sometime after August 1916. Mary O'Hanrahan is the fifth woman from the left sitting in the third row.

Below left and below: Jacob's Biscuit Factory, inside and out.

ꜰɪᴀɴɴᴀ ꜰáɪʟ.
THE IRISH VOLUNTEERS

SERVICE KIT.

The following are the articles prescribed by Headquarters for the personal equipment of Volunteers on field service. Items printed in **heavy type** are to be regarded as important:

FOR ALL VOLUNTEERS.

(a.) As to clothes: uniform or other clothes as preferred; if uniform not worn clothes to be of neutral colour; nothing white or shiny (white collar not to be worn); **soft-brimmed hat** (to be worn in lieu of cap on field service); strong comfortable boots; overcoat.

(b.) As to arms: **rifle,** with sling and **cleaning outfit;** 100 rounds of **ammunition,** with **bandolier** or **ammunition pouches** to hold same; **bayonet,** with scabbard, frog and belt; strong knife or slasher.

(c.) As to provision for rations: **haversack, water-bottle,** mess-tin (or billy can) with knife, fork, spoon, tin cup; 1 dry stick (towards making fire); emergency ration.

(d.) **Knapsack** containing: spare shirt, pair of socks, towel, soap, comb; scissors, needle, thread, safety-pins.

(e.) In the pocket: clasp-knife, note-book and pencil, matches in tin box, boot laces, strong cord, a candle, **coloured** handkerchiefs.

(f.) Sewn inside coat: **First Field Dressing.**

FOR OFFICERS.

(a.) As to clothes: uniform is very desirable for officers; if not worn   sufficient but not unduly conspicuous distinguishing mar¹   ᶠ rank to be worn.

(b.) ᴢ   ᵃ arms: **automatic pistol** or **revolver,** with **ammunition** for sa   e, in lieu of rifle; sword, sword bayonet, or short lance.

The rest ꜰf the equipment as for ordinary Volunteers, with the following

(c.) Additions: **Whistle** on cord; **Watch; Field Despatch-book;** Fountain Pen or **Copying-ink Pencil;** Field-Glasses; Pocket Compass; Range Finder; **Map** of District; electric torch, hooded.

Sub-Officers and **Scouts** should as far as possible be provided with the additional articles prescribed for Officers

By Order

The Equipment Order ꜰꜰ the Irish Volunteers

Headquarters instructions for equipment for Officers and Men of the Irish Volunteers.

Above: One of the 1,500 German Mausers Model 1871 smuggled into Howth and Kilcoole in 1914 and used during the 1916 Rising.

Below: Two bayonets and a Volunteer belt buckle found in the burnt-out ruins of the GPO in 1916.

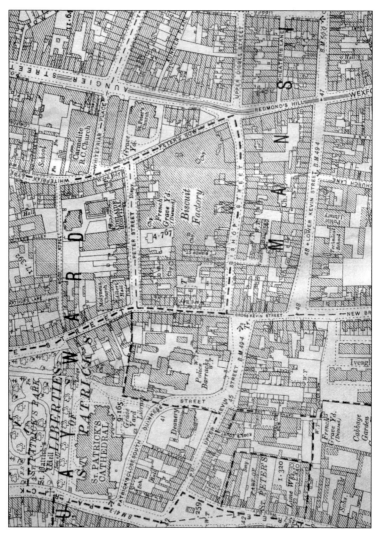

A map of the area surrounding Jacob's Biscuit Factory.

be down due to the holiday season, to September. This ultimately proved to be a mistake, because the association of
the parade with the St Patrick's Day holiday gave it a much
greater impact than it could hope to achieve on an autumn
date, and eventually the parade was moved back to March.

That the procession nevertheless continued to be a major
event for the Gaelic League in 1908 and 1909 was in part
thanks to the efforts of Miceál Ua hAnnracáin, a regular at
the meetings of the All-Ireland Demonstration Committee
(which was chaired by Eoin MacNeill).

If Miceál had not previously been mentioned in the files of
Dublin Castle, he would have come to the attention of British intelligence as a result of the 1908 language procession
booked in his name. A large crowd assembled at the Gaelic
League's headquarters in Rutland Square and marched as a
three-mile-long procession, taking about fifty minutes to
pass any particular point, meaning that it was about 30,000
strong. Miceál, alongside Pádraic Mac Giolla Iosa, helped
arrange the speakers and plan the order of the march as well
as organise the marshals stewarding the event.[46]

By 1909, a great deal of the planning of the procession
lay in Miceál's hands. For example, on 10 September 1909,
he was asked to deal with a last-minute crisis. After being
guaranteed £42, the Great Northern Railway Company had
agreed to put on a special train to Dublin from Belfast, taking
in Omagh, Enniskillen, Oldcastle and Kells. But the com-

pany refused to advertise this train. Therefore, the committee decided to print up 1,000 bills and, through their own efforts, promote the train in the north. The full responsibility for this was given to Miceál Ua hAnnracáin. Furthermore, the distribution of posters advertising the demonstration in and about Dublin was also left to Miceál and he was directed to get an ass and cart to advertise through the streets of the capital.[47] The march was another huge success, with its main message being that the Irish language should be an essential subject at matriculation. Excursion trains from all parts of the country brought huge crowds to Dublin, perhaps more attended than ever before because Sackville Street (O'Connell Street) was completely full of people listening to speeches from three platforms erected along the centre.[48]

During his early years in Dublin, Miceál often enjoyed the hospitality of Jennie Wyse Power. The Powers frequently gave picnics – every Sunday in the summer – by a stream in a forest a short distance beyond Cruagh, Rathfarnham, in the Dublin Mountains. Among the couple of dozen people who were invited to these outings were the O'Hanrahan brothers and Eily.[49]

Although Miceál was the most politically active member of his family – what with the GAA, the Gaelic League and Sinn Féin, he barely had an evening at home – his brothers and sisters (with the exception of Edward, in Carlow) were fully with him on the same political path. Eily O'Hanrahan, for example, in October 1905, sang to warm applause at the Large Concert Hall of the Rotunda, in aid of the O'Donovan Rossa Testimonial Fund.[50] The O'Hanrahan sisters were members of the Red Hugh O'Donnell Branch of the precursor to Sinn Féin, Cumann na nGaedheal, and that branch assisted in providing Christmas treats (toys, fruit, cakes, etc.) to three hundred children of the North Dock. This was a much-appreciated occasion that drew heartfelt thanks to the O'Hanrahan sisters.[51]

During the elections to Dublin Corporation in 1907, the O'Hanrahan sisters came to support Paul Gregan's candidature meeting on Wednesday 1 January 1907 at the National Workers' rooms, 48 Talbot Street. Gregan, a theosophist alongside WB Yeats, Count Plunkett and Æ, committed himself to Sinn Féin and at the meeting gave a particular thanks to the sisters for the excellent work they had done.[52]

Dublin's main *céili* took place every December shortly after Christmas, and in 1909 the O'Hanrahan sisters were heavily involved in organising it, as they were members of the Wolfe Tone Memorial Committee, which took responsibility for the event. The treasurer of the committee and someone with whom the O'Hanrahans exchanged communications on an almost daily basis was Tom Clarke.[53] The family were rapidly moving towards the centre of radical nationalist activity in Dublin.

Chapter 6

The Novelist

As with many other leaders of the Easter Rising, Miceál Ua
hAnnracáin was passionate about Irish literature, both as
a reader and a writer. Whereas his literary colleagues turned
to poetry or drama for the stage, Miceál harboured a desire to
write novels. But he was effectively a full-time revolutionary,
with few evenings to spare: for of all the literary art forms,
writing novels requires the greatest investment of time. Only
at the completion of the novel – perhaps several years' work
– can the aspirant writer judge whether his or her work has
been a success; the learning curve for writing novels is therefore a slow one. In Miceál's case, he worked on his major literary achievement, the novel *A Swordsman of the Brigade* (1914),
for at least nine years, for his friend Harry Phibbs remembered
Miceál speaking of writing an Irish romantic novel in 1905
and spending some time in the National Museum studying
the uniforms of the Irish Brigade.[1] Francis P Jones, a friend of
Arthur Griffith's at the time that Miceál was working for the

newly formed Sinn Féin, recalled that, 'O'Hanrahan became possessed of an ambition to write. He plunged into a course of study that developed his faculties and rapidly advanced him to the rank of a man of letters ... He was of a retiring disposition, and spent a great deal of his time at home, reading far into the night books of Irish verse and Irish history, romances of the Golden Age, and tales of the myths and legends of Éirinn.'[2]

Although reading, studying, writing and attending literary events as often as he could in the early years of the twentieth century, it was not until 1914 that Miceál Ua hAnnracáin's first creative writing was published, with the short story 'Patches' appearing in *The Catholic Bulletin*, Volume IV.1 (January 1914). Written in the omniscient voice, like many works aimed at young people in that era, the narration is that of a kindly, if slightly condescending, older person. The story is that of a poor working-class labourer, Art Maloney, who lives with his wife and son, who is about nine years of age, in a cottage in East Wall, Dublin. Along with his school-fellows, Art's son is allowed the afternoon off to participate in 'School Day' at the Grand Continental Circus, though it was difficult enough for Art 'to spare out of his meagre wages the two pence which brought his little boy to the circus'.

Having become infatuated with Patches the clown, with a passion that modern children invest in sports stars, Art's son falls sick from a chill, brought on while waiting in hope of seeing his hero. It is touch-and-go whether the boy will live, with the doctor saying he must be given a reason to rally. Knowing his son's main enthusiasm in life, Art overcomes his reluctance to push himself on a celebrity like Patches and goes to see the clown. The critical moment comes after Art explains that his child is at death's door.

'And you wish that I should go to him. Is that it?' asked the clown.

'Ah, sir, if you only would. He's only a little fellow, our only child. And maybe you have a little boy yourself.'

For an instant the clown turned away. When he turned again his rubicund face was pale, and he spoke in a soft, subdued voice which trembled slightly.

'Aye, I had once.' His eyes had a far-away, dreamy look, and he seemed not be aware of the other's presence. Perhaps he gazed into the long gone past to a cot where a little child with golden curls lay gasping in the throes of diphtheria. But he roused himself.

'Come,' he said to Art. 'We'll see what Dr Patches can do.'

Given that diphtheria was incurable until 1890 and that it, along with other respiratory infections, was all too common in Dublin's slums in the early twentieth century, Miceál Ua hAnnracáin's story would have evoked genuine pathos in the reader. For example, Tom Clarke would have recalled the experience of his own son, Daly, catching diphtheria in

1903, aged three years old. Daly survived the illness, but hundreds of Irish children a year succumbed to it.[3]

'Patches' is reprinted in this book as an appendix; the reader can form his or her own judgement on it. In order to gauge the worth of the story in a contemporary context, a comparison with James Joyce's writings at the time is worth making. Such a comparison is unfair – Miceál did not have the same education nor the time to devote himself to literature as did Joyce – nevertheless, since 'Patches' is of comparable length to Joyce's stories in *Dubliners* and since it concerns characters in the same city and in the same period, the exercise is useful in obtaining a measure of Miceál Ua hAnnracáin as a literary figure.

Interestingly, the difference between Joyce and Miceál Ua hAnnracáin at this time is not particularly one of technique. Although the modernist revolution in the arts was underway (with literature lagging a little behind music and the visual arts), it would take the experience of the Great War to create a true watershed between modern and nineteenth century styles of writing. In terms of its narrative method, *Dubliners* shows no intimations of *Ulysses,* let alone *Finnegans Wake.* Both these authors told their tales in similar voices. The real difference between them is in fact more a psychological and moral one than a technical one.

Joyce's stories are far darker than 'Patches' and the darkness comes not from the circumstances of the protagonists but from their souls. Miceál Ua hAnnracáin chose to write of characters whose poverty was of a more desperate order than the lower–middle–class characters predominant in Joyce, but Miceál's story is not dark; if anything, it is in danger of becoming saccharine in its depiction of the kindly natures of all concerned. It is a comfortable story, and no reader of *The Catholic Bulletin* would have been troubled by it. By contrast, *Dubliners* is a very troubling book that would have enraged many of the same readers with its candid acknowledgement of the existence of a Dublin population preoccupied by sex, anger, status, violence, atheism and so forth.

In the same year as 'Patches' (1914) came the publication of *A Swordsman of the Brigade* by Sands of Edinburgh. *Swordsman* was a book of 231 pages and cost 3s. 6d. It was given a red cloth cover, lettered in white on the spine and the front cover, with the design of a sword pointing upwards also on the cover. The spine, mistakenly, has 'Michael' for 'Micheal' O hAnnrachain, the version of Miceál's name inside the cover. The IRB newspaper *Irish Freedom* announced the imminent publication of *Swordsman* in its November 1914 issue and no doubt would have carried a review of the novel but for the suppression of the newspaper after the December issue. The book was serialised in *Sinn Féin* late in 1914 and into 1915.

An accurate and contemporary overview of *Swordsman* is provided by Stephen Brown, founder of the Central Catholic Library. Brown edited a guide to Irish literature, which was updated regularly. The IRB were enthusiastic about Brown's work and in general with the value of nation-building through the creation of a distinct body of writing by Irish authors, with *Irish Freedom* stating this in its launch edition of November 1910. The updated edition of Brown's compilation, *Ireland in Fiction,* published in 1916, describes *Swordsman* as 'a fine stirring adventure story of the doings of one of the "Wild Geese": in Sheldon's division of the Irish Brigade in the service of France. Scene: Flanders, Bavaria, Italy and Dublin. *c.*1693. Told in a breezy way and thoroughly Irish in spirit.'[4]

Historically, exiles from Ireland had been fighting as distinct units in the French army since 1635, their numbers rising and falling according to the outcome of battles and political struggles in Ireland. After King Louis XIV of France made peace with Britain in 1697, his Irish troops were reorganised and the cavalry regiment became known after its colonel proprietor, Dominic Sheldon. The adventures of these Irish warriors provided the country with a literary tradition of lively tales that were the equivalent of the American Western. By 1914, popular titles concerning the Irish Brigade included Maria Edgeworth's *Ormond* (Macmillan, Dent & Co., 1817), Lily MacManus's *Lally of the the Brigade* (Duffy, 1899) and *The House of Lisronan* (Melrose, 1912) by Miriam Alexander (Mrs Stokes).[5] This last book was very popular, selling six editions in less than two months and win-

ning a 250 guinea prize. Its success may have helped Miceál
find a publisher for his own manuscript.

One potential hazard for the historical novelist is that
in researching the period in which his or her tale is set, a
desire can grow to communicate history rather than to write
a novel. The problem with reading history as an aesthetic
experience, however, is that all too often the development of
actual events and personalities is chaotic. Rivalries develop
but then peter out without resolution; characters come and
go; schemes are launched but not realised until long after the
death of those who originated them, and so forth. Moreover,
the interpretation of history is always contested, and treating
a particular well-known historical person either favourably
or unfavourably is likely to alienate readers with the opposite
perspective. Making a sensible choice, therefore, in *Swordsman*, Miceál avoided dealing too much with actual historical
personalities or events, but rather used the background of the
period to write a dashing tale of duels, imprisonment, escape
and daring escapades.

The novel is the first-person account of Piaras Grás, son
of an Irish nobleman ruined by the Penal Laws, who flees to
France to join Sheldon's cavalry brigade. Drinker, smoker,
gambler, but venerator of the female sex, Piaras is an attrac-
tive, gallant hero. Although on the whole it is a novel written
in the past tense, by a much older Piaras Grás looking over
his life, Miceál was not afraid to change to present tense to

increase a sense of immediacy for certain scenes. Thus, as Piaras sits smoking opposite the opponent with whom he is about to duel (while surrounded by enemy soldiers and facing certain doom), we read:

> As we smoked we chatted of the engagements we had been in, of the chiefs we had served under, of the many things which interest soldiers. Then he told me of his country, far-away Silesia, and I talked of the gleanns and valleys of Green Eire. Surely men are incomprehensible beings, and to think that in a few moments our swords would seek each other's breasts.
>
> At last we throw away the ends of our cigars, and range out opposite each other. The swords hiss along one another; then with nerves tense, eyes watching every motion, the duel begins.
>
> From the first I saw that I had the advantage. Taller than I, he had the longer reach, but my lightness of foot and swiftness of thrust outmatched his slower, heavier move-ments ...[6]

Changing to the present tense, as he does in the middle paragraph here, is daring but neatly and effectively done. In utilising these kinds of techniques, Miceál was demonstrating a considerable confidence in his writing ability and the novel has a modern flavour thanks to such devices.

With regard to a second technical question, however, the

novel is a little less successful. There are some advantages to adopting a narrative that looks back over the story from a later date. An important one is that the reader accepts that the narrator is in a position to construct a coherent account. Also, from such a standpoint the author can have the narrator editorialise for the sake of suspense. A passage that might otherwise seem to be a fairly pedestrian link between scenes is much more interesting if the author signals that it is, in fact, portentous. Only in retrospect can a narrator write lines such as: 'But if I could have foreseen the other fateful consequences which were to spring from that unfortunate meeting, I never would have …' In *Swordsman* Miceál Ua hAnnracáin makes full use of the opportunity to make such editorial interjections from the informed narrator. The disadvantage of this perspective, however, is that unless the narration turns out to be from a dead person, the reader knows that the narrator must survive every danger in order to tell the tale. This is a major problem for a book like *Swordsman,* which relies so heavily on near-death encounters for its tension.

Miceál's method of addressing this problem is to write at times as though the narrator, Piaras Grás, is abruptly immersed in the moment and has no foreknowledge of the outcome. This lack of knowledge as to what will happen next is particularly evident when, for example, Piaras mistakenly thinks that a beautiful young woman, Aimée Neffer, has betrayed him. The consequent clash between voices – between a man looking back at his past versus one living in the moment – is jarring and is ultimately the reason why, although *A Swordsman of the Brigade* is a good, enjoyable read, it does not hold a high place in the canon of Irish literature.

From the point of view of Miceál's participation in the Easter Rising, there are some interesting moments in the book. Piaras returns to Ireland to recruit for the brigade. Should he be caught, he will be hung. But 'the administrators of the law seemed to be blissfully unconscious of my presence, and the people were true. I came and went without let or hindrance as if never a Government existed.'[7] By misleading his opponents, Piaras is able to successfully ensure that his recruits to the brigade safely embark on a ship from Howth, right under the eyes of the authorities. This whole section of the novel is very evocative of the experience of being a dedicated revolutionary working secretly in an imperially controlled Dublin, and it seems likely that Miceál was successfully turning his life experience into art.

There might also be an echo of personal experience in Piaras's meditation on the ethics of inviting a woman to love him when he was facing almost certain exile, imprisonment or death:

> Seated beside her I felt myself almost carried away by the passionate love which surged through my veins. I was sorely tempted to pour out the burning words which would put

my fate to the test. But honour held me back. Even though I was convinced that her answer would be the fulfillment of all my hopes, what right had I, an adventurer, a soldier engaged in such a dangerous game, to speak of love to her? Living a double life, would it be worthy of me to offer her my love? What right had I to entangle her free, joyous existence with my wayward fate? No! Love was not for me, and I put the temptation from me.[8]

In a letter to 'Quartermaster' at Dawson Street in October 1915 (and therefore probably to Miceál), Cork Sinn Féin founder-member and trade unionist Tadhg Barry joked that with two sisters they knew having entered a convent, 'evidently we had greater effect on them than we thought'.[9] Other than this light teasing, there is no record of Miceál's relationships beyond friends and family. Although he was immersed in a lively social milieu – all the various nationalist organisations he was involved in had their céilithe and literary events – Miceál kept the affairs of his heart even more secret than his rebel activities. It may well have been that Miceál's own thoughts on love followed those of his narrative voice in *Swordsman*.

As we will see later, Miceál Ua hAnnracáin would go on to lecture Cumann na mBan on the topic of Irish heroines. Here, it is worth noting that women are portrayed in *Swordsman* rather as he portrays them historically; that is, in a contradictory fashion where on the one hand their actual deeds

111

are magnificent but on the other, it is taken for granted that they are the weaker sex, psychologically as well as physically. Thus, in terms of her actions, Aimée Neffer is portrayed as courageous, quick-thinking and resourceful. Yet she has these lines: 'And I had thought that I was brave, but I see now that I am only a weak girl, affrighted by a little danger. Ah, mon ami, what risks you are running for my sake.' And later, 'Ah, what a burthen I am,' she cried. 'Only a poor, weak girl.'[10] This last speech comes from a passage where, in order for Miceál to arrive at a scene where Piaras bravely holds off the chasing enemies, Aimée has to be described as being too frail to hurry up a mountainside, needing to be carried much of the way. This very much clashes with the knowledge we are given that she lives among the heights as a mountaineer, a daughter of a rebel chief.

All of the O'Hanrahans were devout Catholics and – in addition to the generally pervasive sexist notions of the early twentieth century – it might well be that the church's outlook on the role of women influenced Miceál's writings. There is more than a hint that this might be the case in Fr Michael O'Flanagan's praise for *Swordsman*. 'To read it is like drinking from a pure mountain stream. There is a little love in it, the love of a decent Irish boy for a pure, high-minded Irish girl. But the principal interest in the story lies in the adventures of an Irish soldier in the Irish Brigade – the real Irish Brigade – in France and in Ireland.' (Fr O'Flanagan went on to praise the book in terms that might have been more appropriate for reviewing an instruction manual: 'The book has one quality at least that is a mark of what is greatest in literature. It is easily understood. There is not a sentence in it that one must puzzle over in order to guess the author's meaning.')[11]

Swordsman was a modestly successful book and of course it had particular appeal to Miceál's comrades in the struggle for independence. His friend and fellow officer in the Second Battalion of the Dublin Brigade of the Irish Volunteers, Thomas MacDonagh, gave the novel a very positive review in *The Catholic Bulletin* of July 1915.

Serious difficulties are presented to the reviewer by the romance of the Irish Brigade recently published by Captain Michael O hAnnrachain of the Irish Volunteers. It lacks the complexity, the plot, of most modern novels. It is worth a hundred of them. It is a Gaelic novel in English. It has, comparatively, no Anglicizing influence. It is published in Scotland – all praise to the enterprise of the publisher. It is addressed solely to the Irish people. To them it has a meaning and a message. It has more – the Gaelic spirit of that time of the Wild Geese, so much nearer to the spirit of European chivalry than to the alien English civilization with which it was at war – the Gaelic spirit that, in the disasters of the following time, shrank back and grew all but silent; but which in this day and in books like this speaks out again with pride. For the book is one of a select class in this respect. The Irish language is taken for granted, as French, say, is taken for granted by English novelists. Names and phrases in Gaelic stand untranslated and unashamed. No Irishman will make a difficulty of them, and the author is obviously not concerned with others. Irish is not, indeed, scattered at random over the pages: it would be fairer to say that the book reads like a translation of Irish narrative and dialogue, in which the more passionate phrases refuse to change their idiom and rhythm.

'I am content,' she said. '*Dia go deo leat I mbaile agus I gcéin.* Kiss me, Muiris, before I go.'

Passages like this read quite naturally in the story. Our only regret – and the author should take it as a compliment – is that the whole is not left in Irish.

The romance is a series of episodes which may be read separately, each of them having a unity of its own. The author knows his history and has caught the atmosphere of the life of the time. The book is full of military adventure with slight love interest – a manly, healthy story of the Gael by a Gael. The best present you can give a boy or girl is a copy of this romance – you can steal a read of it yourself first.

Although very enthusiastic about promoting the book in society at large, MacDonagh was not so pleased to see it for sale at Volunteer rifle practice. As brigade musketry instructor TJ Meldon recalled: 'While Thomas MacDonagh was yet captain of "C" Company, Second Battalion, Michael

O'Hanrahan, our company treasurer and later Brigade quarter-master, brought out his book *A Swordsman of the Brigade*, several copies of which were on the table at the entrance to the hall in 25 Parnell Square, where miniature rifle practice was being carried on. Thomas MacDonagh, on entering, took a copy of the book and later when addressing the company, referred to the book and its author, mentioning that though the book was worthy of support it was not now time for works of fiction as all our spare time and money should be invested in military text books and other accessories for the coming struggle.'[12]

In the aftermath of the Rising, Miceál's family obtained copies of *Swordsman,* which they sold at their shop and advertised in the press. Copies were sent around the country, post free, for 3s.10d.[13] Unfortunately, the frequency of British and subsequently Free State raids on their premises destroyed the stock of books. At the end of 1941 – beginning 29 December – Radio Éireann broadcast a serialisation of *Swordsman*, narrated by actor (and later TV director) Gerard Healy.[14] Copyright having lapsed on the work, it can now be downloaded and read as an e-book for free from a number of online sources.

Aiming at a youthful readership, Miceál wrote another historical novel, *When the Norman Came,* which was not published until after his execution. In 1918, it appeared in a sturdy, dark-green, cloth-bound edition courtesy of Maunsel & Company, who had become the publishers through which prominent Volunteers, executed or imprisoned, had their writings issued. It was Maunsel, for example, who published Patrick Pearse's collected works as well as an anthology: *Poets of the Insurrection*.

Maunsel were therefore the natural publishers for Miceál Ua hAnnracáin's manuscript. Moreover, since their foundation in 1905, they had become the pre-eminent publishers of Irish literature, acquiring an international standing with the production of a beautiful, gilt-edged, four-volume anthology of the works of JM Synge. In addition to publishing the leading figures of the Irish literary revival – writers such as Lady Gregory, Douglas Hyde, Eva Gore-Booth and Austin Clarke – Maunsel also published radical Irish writing, bringing out, among other titles, James Connolly's *Labour in Irish History* (1910), Æ's *The National Being* (1916) and Sean O'Casey's *The Story of the Irish Citizen Army* (1919). One writer they missed, however, was James Joyce. Despite having bought *Dubliners* and being contracted to publish the book in 1911, the main driving force of the publishing house, the former Belfast coal and shipping businessman George Roberts, delayed its production. Roberts objected to a description of Queen Victoria as the King's 'bloody old bitch of a mother'. In bitter frustration at his treatment by Maunsel, Joyce composed a notorious satire on Roberts, *Gas from a Burner* (1912), which belittled the output of the company and included these lines:

I printed the table-book of Cousins
Though (asking your pardon) as for the verse
'Twould give you a heartburn on your arse:
I printed folklore from North and South
By Gregory of the Golden Mouth:
I printed poets, sad, silly and solemn:
I printed Patrick What-do-you-Colm:
I printed the great John Milicent Synge
Who soars above on an angel's wing
In the playboy shift that he pinched as swag
From Maunsel's manager's travelling-bag.
But I draw the line at that bloody fellow,
That was over here dressed in Austrian yellow,
Spouting Italian by the hour
To O'Leary, Curtis and John Wyse Power.

While Roberts' treatment of Joyce was inexcusable, on the whole Maunsel & Company played a vital role in promoting Irish literature and giving an international platform to many of the poets, playwrights and novelists who were deeply involved in the Easter Rising. Given the radical nationalist politics of Miceál Ua hAnnracáin and the spirit that suffused the novel, it was appropriate that Maunsel commissioned illustrations for *When the Norman Came* from Jack Morrow. A former Belfast illustrator associated with Bulmer Hobson (at some personal risk from stone-throwing crowds, Jack Morrow had displayed political cartoons shown through a magic lantern at the Dungannon Club in 1905), Morrow was in Dublin engaged in drawing nationalist cartoons in 1917 when he composed the images for Miceál Ua hAnnracáin's novel. The eight ink and paper full-page images were competently executed and were of scenes chosen to heighten the drama of the work. Morrow did his best to contrast the noble bearing and looks of the Irish warriors with a less flattering portrait of 'the traitor' MacMurrough and his Norman ally. In the year following publication of *When the Norman Came*, Morrow was arrested on suspicion of involvement with IRA intelligence work.

When the Norman Came opens in 1166, the year that Diarmuid MacMurrough, the king of Leinster, was driven into exile, and it ends in the battle of Scollagh Gap in the Blackstairs Mountains, 1171. It is the story of a young Irish nobleman, Cian MacMurrough, who participates in all the key battles of the era. Told from the perspective of the class who lost most in the invasion, the story nevertheless has a somewhat positive conclusion, as Miceál cleverly chooses to end with the one really successful encounter of Irish troops against Norman soldiers. Moreover, in the aftermath of Scollagh Gap, Cian is shown to have found the love of his life.

In many ways, despite the medieval setting, *When the Norman Came* is a more political novel than *Swordsman*; it sets out to challenge the image of Ireland, which ultimately derives from Gerald of Wales, that the medieval Irish were barbaric. Contemporary literature set in the medieval period, such as the 1908 novel *Let Erin Remember* by NW Knowles (writing as May Wynne), tended to portray Strongbow and the Normans as gentle and courteous knights, while the Irish were wild, murderous and selfish.

There was a strong feeling in the early twentieth century that Ireland's young readers, especially the male ones, deserved a different view of affairs. As Stephen Brown put it at the time: 'That the interest and the discriminating affection of our boys may be won for the Ireland of the present it is necessary that they should have knowledge of her past. And it is surely most desirable that this knowledge should be not merely a matter of intellectual information, such as textbooks supply, but that imagination and feeling, too, should be captured for Ireland. To this end historical novels are undoubtedly a help.'[15] Miceál himself wrote that 'in reading our school books we very often run across vivid pictures of English bravery and magnanimity, so much so that often we are inclined to regret that we, too, were not born English. The exploits of Clive in India – rather the English accounts of his exploits – tend to make young men envy Englishmen. Similarly the accounts of Nelson looking through the telescope with the blind eye, and the charge of the Light Brigade, rouse within us a certain amount of admiration.' He then, however, went on to argue from recent examples, including an horrific punishment of innocent men in Egypt, that despite the tone of such school books England was, in fact, a nation of cowards, 'yet these very same cowards hold in subjection and plunder India, Egypt, and Ireland, and there are men in each to make apologies for and accept "honours" from them. Let our young men be trained that when they grow up they will act otherwise.'[16] It was to offer young Irish readers adventure tales that challenged the myth of English bravery and magnanimity that Miceál wrote *When the Norman Came*.

Stylistically, Miceál Ua hAnnracáin adopted the voice of an omniscient narrator for *When the Norman Came*. Like all novels written in such a fashion, it gives the narrator freedom to visit the minds of multiple characters and to comment on affairs. This is why it was the choice for most nineteenth century novels. For early twentieth century literature it was common enough too – indeed it remains a popular voice in literature to this day – but even at the time there was something archaic about an infallible voice explicating a story: something of the lecture rather than the immersive experience of being in the minds of the protagonists. Miceál was aware of this and even pulled himself up mid-story during the course of a discontented speculation:

> For possibly the strangest feature of the history of the time is the fatal apathy which had gripped the Irish princes. Faced by the danger of a more powerful invasion they did nothing. They seem to have given no attention to the signs and portents, or rather they did not look on the presence of an

English force in the country as the portent of anything serious. They regarded it as nothing more than a mere force of
mercenaries come to the aid of one of their number, which
would be sent away when he required them no longer. Had
they not seen Danish mercenaries employed in like manner
from time to time? Why then trouble about the matter? But
an examination into their motives is rather a matter for the
staid historian, and may not enter into such a story as ours.[17]

Where the style of the book is more lively and daring is in
its somewhat risky attempt to capture a flavour of the times
by adopting an old Irish sentence structure, where an adverb
or adjective begins the sentence. So *When the Norman Came* is
filled with sentences such as 'sharply ring the blows of sword
or battle-axe on the shields'; 'raven-black were the ringlet-
ted locks which fell down on his shoulders from beneath his
crested helmet, inlaid with gold'; 'mournfully the royal herald
gazed on the scene of devastation'; 'loudly his voice rang amid
the din'. Once the reader is acclimatised to this method, it is
very effective and gives the prose a poetic quality and – curi-
ously, since the goal is to suggest the ancient past – a modern
one. Another technical success in Miceál's writing is in the
formulation of passages of considerable sensuality in terms of
their descriptions of the clothing and locations of the period.
For example, in his setting the scene of the fair of Tailtean:

On every side booths and marts had been set up. Here

the Gaulish merchant displayed his wines. There swarthy Moors from the Spanish land had spread out their richly ornamented saddles and horse trappings, beside the meads of some trader from the Muskerrys of Munster. Across the white-capped wave had travelled the citizen of Nantes, with his ornaments of gold and silver, his garments of silk and precious stuffs. Florentines and merchants of Lucca were examining the rich serges and many coloured mantles displayed by the native makers, or fingering the native black wool which required no dye.

In the animal enclosure horse-boys were leading noble colts brought from the Connemara hills, fiery French steeds reared and plunged, while the Welsh dealer had crossed the Sea of Man, bringing with him his trusty British geldings to exchange for the linen and foodstuffs of the Irish land. In booths built of white wattles the native artificers had hung the finest products of their forges and stone-moulds. Here was the heavy broadsword, well-tempered and beautifully wrought. Rows on rows of tall spears attracted the attention of the martially inclined. Bucklers and battle-axes were there. Potters and glass-workers from the Wicklow gleanns showed the choicest specimens of their arts in earthenware and glass worked in enamels. Men who practised the builder's art showed their house-building materials fashioned from the 'chieftain' materials, oak (such oak as the English King William Rufus had imported into his city of London to roof his new Hall at Westminster), hazel and holly.

On every side the sound of music was heard. Round harpers and pipe-players the music-loving people were congregated. Bone-men and castanet-players competed with one another for patronage. But over all rang out the raucous voices of fantastically dressed clowns and gleemen, who by their rude jests and pointed quips, drew shouts of laughter from the bystanders. Balanced erect on the backs of galloping horses, equestrians claimed the plaudits and reward of cheering onlookers.[18]

In piling up vivid description upon vivid description, the result of considerable research, Miceál seems to have been emulating the magnificent *Salammbô* (1862) by Gustave Flaubert. The technique leads to a very clear contrast between the style of writing of his two historical works and suggests that Miceál was becoming more confident and bold as a novelist. He also became more willing to mix past and present tenses, even within the same paragraph, particularly when writing battle scenes. Thus, he took the device he employed in *Swordsman* to good effect and pushed it a little further:

To each of them the king handed a spear, heavy and well-tempered as the *cleitine* of Cuchulainn. Poising himself for an instant on the ball of his foot Cian raises his spear. An instant he pauses taking aim. Then straight and unerring, as an arrow from the bow, it flew through the air, and striking

the shield with tremendous force crashed to the ground, its
point splintered to atoms.[19]

Mixing tenses within a paragraph in such a way can work
to heighten the immediacy of the action, but it can also break
the reader from the spell they are under while engaged with
the book by creating a jarring effect. Changing tenses too
often can create an unnecessarily dislocating reading experience and not all of Miceál's choices in this regard were wise
ones. No editor would have dared touch the manuscript after
Miceál's execution, but had he lived some of these instances
might well have been addressed. There are a few small plot
errors too, suggesting that in an ideal situation the manuscript
would have been redrafted under editorial guidance before
being published.

The events *When the Norman Came* dealt with were the
cause of considerable debate at the time Miceál was writing. Goddard Henry Orpen, an Anglo-Irish County Wexford landlord and Trinity scholar, published the first volume
of his *Ireland under the Normans* in 1911. Provocatively calling his chapter on pre-Norman Ireland 'Anarchic Island',
Orpen's view of the Norman invasion was that it brought
peace and prosperity to an island that had previously been
riven by bitter inter-kingdom feuds. Considering that at
the time of publication one of the main imperial justifications for the rule of Ireland was that the British had played a
civilising mission in a country wracked by internecine war-

fare (a justification that is promulgated still today by leading Oxbridge academics such as Charles Townshend),[20] Orpen's book naturally aroused the wrath of the national movement, whose leading historians hit back with responses such as Eoin MacNeill's *Phases of Irish History* (1920) and with lectures on the Norman invasion, such as that given (for a 3d. ticket) by Arthur Griffith in 25 Parnell Square on 'The English Invasion of 1167'.[21]

The alternative paradigm created by the Irish-Ireland perspective was that the Normans were thuggish brutes who used their military superiority to dispossess their more sophisticated neighbours in Sicily, Southern Italy and Ireland. The pre-Norman Irish world that appeared in these histories emphasised the genuinely impressive achievements of the Irish nobility in regard to their legal and literary culture. Life, however, was not all rosy in twelfth century Ireland, especially for the slaves who toiled at minding the cattle herds and at producing butter and cheese.[22] But the romantic nationalist perspective on historical events always had a blind spot for the lot of the lower social classes, a point that James Connolly made forcefully in his intervention to these debates, *Labour in Irish History*.

When the Norman Came generally adopts the MacNeill/Griffith view of the period, but the invaders are not all villains and thugs, nor are all the Irish heroes. In fact, the most despicable characters in the novel are both Irish: Diarmuid

MacMurrough and the 'Ard-ri' (High King) of Ireland, Rory O'Connor. Diarmuid is simply a Judas figure, named 'traitor MacMurrough' throughout the book, without explanation or justification, and as a result is aesthetically and historically bland; he's just bad. Rory O'Connor, on the other hand, is portrayed in a more interesting fashion, one that would have immediately recalled to contemporary readers figures such as O'Connell or Redmond. He is depicted as a leader of the country who, despite being in command of an enormous body of followers, prevaricates in the face of hard decisions and fears initiating decisive action.

> Again the Ard-ri had marched forth in all his might, but in his might he marched away again. Great in conception, he failed in accomplishment. Showy and weak-minded he was little fitted for the exalted position he occupied ... The only wonder is that he was at all times able to gather together such forces. Possibly the ineptitude of the Ard-ri was as great service to the Anglo-Normans as their arms.[23]

As with *Swordsman*, there are passages in *When the Norman Came* that are very suggestive of Miceál's own concerns. At one point Cian and a Viking friend, Torgil, discuss the problem that while the Irish and their allies have only woollen clothes, the Normans have steel coats. 'None but brave men,' says Cian, 'would oppose themselves to men so much better armed than themselves ... To win against them we must, I fear me, adopt arms and iron coats like them.'[24] This, from an author who at the time of writing was doing his best to acquire arms for the Volunteers, seems to reflect Miceál's own conversations.

Another scene is grimly prophetic. Two Norman leaders, Raymond Le Gros and Hervey de Montmaurice, are arguing over the fate of their captured prisoners, with Hervey winning the debate in favour of executions with the following speech: 'We must employ the victory which has given those men into our hands to strike terror into others. By the execution of these men we must give warning of the fate which awaits those who oppose us.'[25] The response of the Irish prisoners:

> 'We pay the forfeit, Conn,' whispered a warrior whose head was bound around with a bloody bandage. 'We have fought our last fight, I fear.'
>
> 'There is little doubt of that,' returned his fellow-prisoner, a tall Gaedheal, whose right arm hung useless by his side. 'We have no mercy to expect from these foreigners. But they shall not hear me crave for mercy.'
>
> 'Nor me,' growled the first speaker.[26]

As we shall see, Miceál faced his own court-martial and execution with as equal a stoicism as the Irish warrior characters he had created on the page.

When the Norman Came was a great success among young Irish readers and – along with the works of Charles Joseph Kickham (1828–1882), Patrick Augustine Sheehan

(1852–1913) and others – in time helped replace Dickens, the Brontes and Jane Austen in the Irish school system with novels written by Irish authors.[27] The overall strength of the story, despite its minor weaknesses, means that Francis P Jones's judgment seems to be a fair one, that 'in losing O'Hanrahan, Ireland lost an author who would have given her youth many volumes of inspired romance if he had lived'.[28]

A third substantial literary publication by Miceál Ua hAnnracáin was the lecture 'Irish Heroines', which was composed for the Ard Craobh of Cumann na mBan in the winter of 1915. It was published by Miceál's family in 1917, that is, from their shop at 384 North Circular Road, Dublin, where it was for sale as a pamphlet. The printers were also family members, from Wexford.

In his introductory remarks on the subject of Ireland's heroines, Miceál wrote that true heroism was manifest in a person for whom heroic deeds were but duties well performed and not of particular merit, and this thought certainly resonates with his own activites.[29] The structure of the lecture was that of a chronological journey through Ireland's history, highlighting extraordinary deeds by Irish women. An early example was that of the women of New Ross who in 1643 assisted Captain Arthur Fox and 1,500 soldiers who resisted the Duke of Ormond, Lord Lisle and three parliamentary ships that attacked the town. Miceál's presentation was almost entirely literary in its appeal to his listeners to visualise the scene: 'We can imagine those daughters of Ireland standing amidst those hurtling shells and whizzing bullets undauntedly hurling back the attackers. We may imagine them seizing pike or musket, or *sgian* at the sound of the alarm bell and rushing from their homes to take their places where duty called. Poor they may have been, unlettered, but of whatever rank in life, they were heroines.'[30]

A similar example given in the talk was that of the women of the siege of Limerick ('Luimneach') on 27 August 1690, when William's army was cleverly trapped in a narrow breach by the defenders and suffered about 3,000 casualties. Again Miceál offered his listeners a dramatic reconstruction:

A loud vengeful yell swells out above the din of clashing arms, the spiteful snap of pistols, the clang of steel on steel. Across the air it floats, drowning out the oaths, the cries, the shrieks of contending men. Mingling with the deeper notes of men are heard the shriller voices of women. Like a torrent comes sweeping along those men and women fresh from their daily labours. From Mungret Street and Palmerston Street, from the lanes and alleys lying round St John's Church they rush. Croabhach Lane, Fish Lane and many another sends forth its denizens to join in that headlong charge to the breach.

Strange and varied are the weapons they bear, evidently

caught up in the mad excitement of the moment. Here a brawny smith flourishes his ponderous sledge-hammer. There beyond a butcher fresh from the shambles rushes along, waving aloft his reeking pole-axe. See that woman yonder! Naught of weapons has she save her bare hands and a práiscín filled with stones and broken bottles. Beside her pants a woman, her face stern and determined, a stout bludgeon gripped in her hand. Against the foe they hurl themselves, mingling with their soldiers who, reinforced in such timely fashion, force back their antagonists. These women of Luimneach shirked not the fight, but shoulder to shoulder and foot to foot gave back blow for blow.

Slowly the shades of evening fall. The last rays of the expiring sun lights up that bloody breach, and falls across the path of the fleeing Williamites. It falls across the bodies of many a maid and matron of Luimneach who has given her life for Ireland. Mo Bhrón! Mo Bhrón! Many a one of them have fallen before the steel of the foe. Here we behold a fair-haired girl, a smile of peace on her face, her golden tresses dappled with blood, locked in the embrace of death. This is a black-haired woman, a poor, quiet citizeness who had lived her life simply and well. Now she sleeps here, her duty done, her last great sacrifice made.[31]

This type of literary presentation was – and is – most unusual for a political lecture and was no doubt enjoyed as such by the audience. And Miceál was even more colourful when he arrived, via Isabella, the wife of William Orr, to the scenes at New Ross in 1798.

> The town is New Ross. Outside the walls a tall young man is marshaling his men for desperate attack on the gate. He falls, a bullet in his thigh. Then out from the town gallops a strong squadron of the 5th Dragoon Guards, who charge furiously at the patriots. But they are met by the long, bright pike and fall back in confusion, leaving twenty-eight of their number behind them. At this point the heroic Mary Doyle comes into view. She had accompanied the patriots in all their marchings and counter-marchings, borne their fatigues and disappointments as bravely as any stout son of Bargy or Forth or Shilmalier there. Now walking amongst the fallen soldiers she cuts off their cross-belts and cartouche boxes and hands them to her comrades, cheering them on to the combat.
>
> Again we see this intrepid woman in the evening of that day. Begenal Harvey has ordered a retreat to be sounded and the patriots, dispirited by their ill-success, begin to stream away from the town where they have fought and lost. Seeing the weary men abandoning a gun they had brought with them that morning the spirited woman seated herself on it and declared that if 'they did not bring her dear little gun with them she would remain behind also at all risks'. And so 'twas done. The men gave her their assistance to remove her favourite.[32]

Up to this point, *Irish Heroines* is a demonstration 'that heroism is not confined to sex, that it is differentiated only in its quality. Neither is it the prerogative of class or creed, for I have spoken to you of princesses and peasants, of Northern Presbyterian and Southern Catholic, of the women of the people, of great high-born ladies.'[33] In its research and presentation, the talk (and pamphlet) was highly successful in this respect and furnished neglected examples in favour of the argument for equality within the revolutionary nationalist movement. What followed, however, rather contradicted the evidence just presented. As Miceál moved away from the specific examples to make generalised points about gender, his thinking was dominated by the typical assumptions of his day, despite his intention to be positive about women's roles. As a result, there was no question for Miceál (in contradiction to his own examples) that there would be a gender-based division of roles in the coming fight.

> Man cast in rougher mould cannot understand, however much he may sympathise with, the flutterings of the heart of a poor weak woman who sees her men treading the path of danger. He cannot (I speak in general terms) understand the love which dictates her tears. For that reason he is impatient of them, he disregards them only as the expressions of cowardice or self-interest. But no, 'tis not that. True, in some cases it may be that those tears are the sign of self-interest. But not in all, not even in a majority. When danger's hours is nigh,

when the enemy threatens, we see those very women arming their men for the strife, bidding them go forth to conquer or die; shaming the laggards; all the while that the poor, gentle heart trembles for the safety of the loved one and unshed tears may blind the eyes. We see those weak women performing tasks the most daring, with never a thought of fear.

But wailing women have not been a very numerous tribe in our land. Rather have we had a train of courageous women who nerved the arms of their men to strike the needful blow. Our women have not been less brave than our men. They have shown their bravery on the battle-field, and can point to the deeds of a Mary Doyle, a Betsy Gray, the women of Luimneach. But yet the rude shock of war is not for women. To man belongs that duty. To woman, gentle woman, belongs the privilege of binding up the wounds, of living, of mourning. Of living that the race may be saved from extinction. Of mourning the true men who have fallen, and in mourning, carrying on the tradition of lofty duty to their children.

No, women's is a nobler task. Man falls, but the woman lives on in heart-breaking loneliness and gloom, waiting, listening for the voice of him, the lover of her youth, the father of her children, the son of her bosom, he who may not come again. Which is the greater heroism? Is the heroism of Matilda Tone less self-sacrificing than that of the man she sent from her side, telling him that she would watch over their children? She could have bidden him stay, yet she did not. The one heroism, that of the man, who, sword in hand, smites down his enemies, and perhaps is stricken down, is performed when the blood leaps madly through the veins. The other, in the loneliness of the long, sad days, the watches of the dreary nights. Let each one find the answer. 'Tis not far to seek.

How can we poor, everyday people, children of those heroines of whom I have spoken, fit ourselves to be their worthy heirs? Presumptuous it may be on my part to put such a question. Foolish to attempt a reply. But since our Irish-speaking people hold that even a fool has sense, and the Bible tells us that wisdom comes from the mouth of babes, I have resolved to boldly front the charges. And remember, my friends, that I do not claim originality for those teachings of mine. Teaching we have plenty to point us the way. I am but a voice catching up the echoes which come from afar off, the echoes of the voices of other, greater men and women …

The divine spark has descended into the bosom of every woman who does her duty well, who teaches those over whom she has control to work for the fatherland's welfare, regardless alike of the rewards of sycophancy or selfishness. It may be that she will never stand forth in history's pages, her name sent down to future ages, a heroine. But never mind. Of all those who die in the odour of sanctity, how many are called saints? Of all those who perform their duty well by their country, how many will be called heroines? And still will they work on, for their work is necessary. If the world were ruled by the dictates of selfishness, sycophancy, worldliness, the age of heroism, of saintliness would have passed. The good and true may not call them heroines, but they will say they have made heroism possible.

Then to your ladies of Cumann na mBan, I would say: Work, train yourselves for the days to come. Set before yourselves a high standard of duty, of allegiance to this land which God has given us. No other land can claim your allegiance, or will receive it. Her interests are your interests, her wrongs your wrongs. What matters it to us that other empires are great, powerful, rich in this world's goods. We have no double duty, cannot serve two masters. To one country only we owe our love.

Your power is great, women of Ireland. See that you exercise it well. You may be poor, despised, may not own a spadeful of earth. But carry on your tasks, heroically, for it requires heroic qualities to bear up against the sneers and gibes of wordlings and time-servers. Copy the lives of our heroines who stood for the right against might. Strive to be heroines in your daily lives, to be mothers, sisters, lovers of heroes, and when, as we all hope and pray, those days of glorious peace and freedom shall dwell in our land; when we, having borne the heat and burthen of the day, shall gaze on a free flag, a free people, you can whisper in your hearts

we 'fought the good fight; we kept the faith'. And men and
women looking back to your time will whisper in their
hearts: 'These were heroines, every one.'

There were other literary works by Miceál in his house,
but most of these were lost after they were taken by British soldiers in the aftermath of the Rising. As his sister Eily
recalled, 'All Micheál's manuscripts, cuttings from papers that
he had written for, and all such things were seized and never
returned.'[34] In the account by the *Irish Press* of a 1966 anniversary meeting given by Eily, she tantalisingly stated that
although his second novel of the Irish Brigade, *My Sword,
My Fortune,* was taken by the British and never returned, she
had in her possession an unpublished manuscript: *The Life of
Patrick Sarsfield*. It is possible that this book may yet survive
to see publication one day.[35]

When JS Crone cast his eye over the loss to Irish literature
from the executions in *The Irish Book Lover* of October and
November 1916, he wrote of how many promising literary
careers had been sacrificed. Interestingly, valuing non-fiction,
he gave Connolly the greatest credit as an author ('no one
can read his *Labour in Irish History* without recognising its
argumentative force and skill'). MacDonagh was 'beyond
question the most distinguished of the insurgents'; Pearse,
'not so essentially literary as MacDonagh' but a remarkable speaker; Clarke, the author of an account of prison life
better than any other work of this kind. Crone wrote that

he would also 'find a niche for Michael O'Hanrahan'. This praise is rather too faint. Of all the literary figures involved in the Rising, Miceál was the only one to be devoted to the novel as an art form, despite having to cope with enormous demands on his time.

In part, Miceál's dedication to literature sprang from the same source as his drive towards rebellion. For many Irish writers of the early twentieth century, it was important to create Irish characters that defied the all-too-prevalent offensive and negative portrayals of Irish people in British literature. There was a particular dearth of novels for younger readers with positive portrayals of the Irish. In Miceál Ua hAnnracáin's historical novels, this bias is reversed: it is Irishmen who are heroic, and the villains are British or Irish traitors. In principle, there is nothing wrong with this; every nation has its heroic figures and its despicable ones, and by making the choices he did, Miceál was making a small attempt to redress an enormous imbalance. There is a difficulty, however, when the characters lack depth because their behaviour is overdetermined by the plot roles they are required to play.

In Joyce, there appear characters who are riven by contradiction, whose being is driven by their unconscious brain as well as their conscious aims. This early incorporation of the Freudian revolution into literature by Joyce makes for enduring and fascinating reading. In Miceál Ua hAnnracáin's work, by contrast, there is little ambiguity, evolution or shock in the development of his characters. For the most part, they don't develop but are fixed from the outset: hero, villain or traitor. As a young writer, Miceál Ua hAnnracáin was initially limited not by the coherence or immersive quality of his fictional world, which was perfectly well executed, but by his shying away from the disturbing implications of the contradictions of human consciousness. Of course, Miceál's artistic endeavours were cut short and it is impossible to know the writer he would have become if he had lived to devote himself to writing novels.

Not yet forty at the time of his execution, Miceál was rapidly gaining confidence in a variety of literary techniques and no doubt would have studied the post-War experiments in literature with great interest. Had he lived, at the very least Ireland would have enjoyed many more home-grown adventure novels for young adults in which Irishmen and Irishwomen were the heroes and heroines.

Chapter 7

• • • • •

1911-1916

The Volunteer

In the 1911 census, Miceál is listed as an unemployed 'reader for the press'. The rest of the household at 67 Connaught Street consisted of his mother Mary and siblings Harry, Anna, Máire and Eily. Their house and shop had seven rooms, with three windows at the front, putting it into the 'second' class of house.[1] Anna is described as a tobacconist's assistant, indicating in part the nature of the goods they sold at their shop. By this time Harry had found work as an insurance agent and Eily was recorded as being an art student.[2] (Although Eily's passion for art was subordinated to her political activity, she never lost interest in being a painter and at the age of forty-eight, she enrolled in the Metropolitan School of Art, Dublin.[3])

Many activists for the national movement were frequent visitors at 67 Connaught Street, including Con Colbert and Thomas MacDonagh, 'a great friend' of Miceál's.[4] And as we have seen, the family were in regular communication with

the Clarkes. The network of republican activists of which
the O'Hanrahans were a part embarked on a more intensive
period of activity with the formation of the Irish Volunteers
on 25 November 1913. Miceál was one of the delegates who
launched the new movement.[5] Chief-of-Staff of the Volunteers was the UCD professor Eoin MacNeill, someone who
was not a member of the IRB but was willing to take the
lead in creating a new, public military organisation for Irish
nationalists.

Miceál Ua hAnnracáin was an officer for the Volunteers
from the beginning, being secretary of the Second Battalion
of the Dublin Brigade. As with all of the Volunteer battal-
ions, the number of its members steadily grew throughout
1914, until by June of that year the movement as a whole
had over 100,000 members. At that point, John Redmond
thought it necessary to control the new organisation and
forced his supporters onto the leadership of the Volunteers.
This attempt to channel the movement behind his political
strategy resulted only in a split when Redmond announced
the IPP's wholehearted support for Britain at the outbreak
of the Great War. When, on 20 September 1914, Redmond
then urged all Volunteers to join the British war effort, the
original founders of the movement (including Eoin Mac-
Neill) were furious. Those opposed to Redmond split from
the main group of Volunteers – taking the name 'Irish Volunteers' with them – with the intention of restoring an anti-

Imperial spirit to the force. And of course Miceál was among those to participate in the breakaway.

After the split with the Redmondites, a minority of the Dublin Brigade followed the Irish Volunteers, which necessitated a reorganisation of the members. As a result, Miceál was given a role requiring discretion and careful accounting skills, that of battalion quartermaster. This appointment was announced in *The Irish Volunteer* on 20 March 1915. His commandant was Thomas MacDonagh.

As well as his local responsibilities, at around this time Miceál was appointed Executive Official of a sub-committee of the new Volunteer Executive (chaired by The O'Rahilly) that was responsible for the procurement of arms. 'He it was,' recalled Seán T O'Kelly, 'who knew what arms and ammunition had been obtained and where they were stored.'[6]

Effectively a full-time Volunteer worker who daily attended Volunteer headquarters, Miceál became well known to the 'G' men and it was a prominence in their reports that may well have ensured his execution. The Dublin Metropolitan Police kept a man outside of both Tom Clarke's shop and the Volunteer offices, making a note of the movements of 'extremists'. The files the detectives created give Miceál considerable attention due to his frequent appearances both at the shop and the office. Of 251 reports, 125 mention Miceál, making him one of the most notable persons in the police records.[7]

The headquarters of the Volunteers before the split was at 205 Great Brunswick Street (now Pearse Street) near the Queen's Theatre; this was the address given in *The Irish Volunteer* until its edition of 5 December 1914, when a headquarters at 41 Kildare Street was listed.[8] About three weeks after the split – during which time the Kildare Street office was defended by a mobilisation of Na Fianna Éireann and plenty of barbed wire against a possible attempt by the Redmondites to break in – the Executive of the new Irish Volunteers took over 2 Dawson Street, which remained their headquarters up to the Rising.[9] While at Kildare Street, Miceál Ua hAnnracáin was already acting with a wide national remit, for it was on his authority that Daniel Dennehy, IRB member and future captain of Rathmore Company IV, was issued with two hundred rounds of .303 ammunition on Dennehy's trip up to the office from County Kerry.[10]

Number 2 Dawson Street is a three-story building close to the junction of Dawson Street and Nassau Street. In 1916, it was owned by John Hutton & Son, a long-established coach-building firm. They in turn leased the building through the Stephen's Green solicitor's firm Stanuell & Son. The lease was taken for a year on 29 April 1915 and by the end of that year, John Hutton & Son were very anxious to regain the premises. Three letters of increasing severity were sent to 'John' MacNeill demanding confirmation that the Volunteers would vacate the building by 29 April 1916, but of course the question of possession of the premises was completely overshadowed by the Rising, which began five days before the keys were to be handed over.[11]

It was in 2 Dawson Street that Miceál Ua hAnnracáin made his most important contribution to the national movement, for he was in charge of a premises that acted as a key central hub for both the IRB and the Volunteers. On the very top floor was a room for The O'Rahilly, who was chairperson of the armaments subcommittee of the Volunteers[12] and played a role in buying arms and storing them there. On the floor below, Bulmer Hobson, as secretary for the Volunteers, had his room and the assistance of Maeve Ryan (who was well known at the time as a champion Irish dancer). In the office opposite Bulmer Hobson's was Miceál Ua hAnnracáin, while on the ground floor were the clerks and a messenger, Seumas Cooling. As far as Kitty O'Doherty, quartermaster for Cumann na mBan, was concerned, Michael O'Hanrahan managed the headquarters.[13]

In order to commemorate the shootings on Bachelor's Walk on 26 July 1914 (when the King's Own Scottish Borderers shot dead three unarmed people among a crowd that were mocking the soldiers for their failure to stop the Volunteers landing arms that day at Howth), a thick stone plaque was placed on the very threshold to the entrance. It was about three feet by two feet and three or four inches thick. In order to prevent any opponents of the Volunteers removing the stone, it was chained down at the corners and it remained in place until the British Army removed it after the Rising.[14]

As a meeting place, 2 Dawson Street was used for a number of classes in military training, especially in the run-up to the Easter Rising. By day, the building functioned more or less respectably as an office – although in fact it often held arms – and the non-political administrative staff were unaware of its more subversive role. That the really important functions of the building were secret led to problems on the day that Nellie Gifford (Grace's sister and member of the Citizen Army) took it upon herself to set up an employment bureau on the premises for trade unionists and nationalists. On that day, Thomas MacDonagh rang Kitty O'Doherty, saying that Nellie Gifford was running them all mad and for God's sake could Kitty sort things out.[15]

TJ Meldon taught an armourer's class at 2 Dawson Street and regularly met with Thomas MacDonagh on the premises.[16] Meldon had a workshop fitted up at 2 Dawson Street, containing a bench, a large and small vice, an emery wheel and an assortment of suitable tools for the repair of guns.[17] MacDonagh himself gave a series of lectures from the spring of 1915.[18] Signaling classes were held there,[19] and a select group of Volunteers were sent to two special classes on the premises at the end of 1915 and in the early months of 1916: one consisted of lectures on street fighting, and the other, lectures on first aid.[20] 'The lectures were usually given on a Saturday,' remembered Liam O'Carroll, '... I think there were only the Battalion Officers and Captains of Companies attending. Although I was not a Company Captain, I was there; and I was Secretary to the Lectures.'[21]

No doubt with Miceál's connivance, the premises were also used to convene discreet meetings of the IRB. It was at 2 Dawson Street, for example, that Éamon de Valera was taken to be interviewed by MacDonagh for IRB membership the Thursday before the Rising.[22] It was there too that John MacDonagh, brother of Thomas, was sworn in by Éamonn Ceannt one night.[23] Officially, Miceál Ua hAnnracáin was present in 2 Dawson Street as an insurance worker. Unofficially, he was combining the role of national official in charge of weapons procurement with that of quartermaster for his own Second Battalion.

By the end of 1915, if not earlier, Miceál Ua hAnnracáin was acting as Quartermaster General and dealing with national concerns related to that position. Frank McGrath, a Nenagh grocer who was subsequently commandant of the Tipperary No. 1 Brigade, recalled Miceál as being one of the leaders of the Volunteers (along with The O'Rahilly and Cathal Brugha) that he was in close contact with.[24] Similarly, Tomás Ceannt wrote to HQ from Castlelyons in September 1915, saying that he was ...

> ... badly in need of at least ½ doz rifles as I cannot do much without them and I have 8 solid men here and outriders are

under the opinion we are fully armed. If you can possibly do anything for me it would be an immense service to the movement. Mr O'Hanrahan will know who to communicate with. I am after advertising Sunday's meeting by poster and addressed the people coming out from church at both masses last Sunday week. If I will have anything to show in guns I will proceed to organise Conna, Rathconnae, Kilwoth, Glanwoth, Ballyhoody etc soon as possible. In writing you need not mention guns. Mr O'Hanrahan will know.[25]

Miceál was trusted entirely to deal with large amounts of money, whether in regard to transactions that were open to public scrutiny or in regard to the less transparent use of funds needed to procure arms and equipment, such as the gold coins that were smuggled into the country for the movement from America. On one occasion, for example, Pat McCartan returned from New York with £2,000 in gold from Clan na Gael for the IRB.[26] It is testimony to the confidence of his peers in Miceál's honesty and integrity that he was trusted with the handling – in secret and therefore with little accountability – of very large sums of money. Francis P Jones recalls Miceál's growing importance to the Volunteers: 'He gave up a great deal of his literary work to drill and learn the art of soldiering. With the passing of time his enthusiasm became greater, and, as his proficiency increased, he was promoted from one rank to another, until he had gained a prominence that made him a marked man. At the time of the rising he was treasurer of the Arms' Fund and the most trusted man in the organisation.'[27]

The strongest evidence for Miceál's central role in arming the Volunteers is that even before the split with the Redmondites, Miceál had responsibility for the national fund launched on 9 June 1914. As Seamus Ua Caomhanaigh explained to the Military Bureau:

> One day Seamus O'Connor came to me. He was a member of the Executive Committee of the Volunteers. He asked me to take up the position of Secretary of the 'Defence of Ireland Fund'. This was the fund out of which the arms for the Volunteers were to be purchased. I was reluctant to do so but Seamus impressed on me the importance of the work and as I was not doing very well at the time I took it on. The work consisted of receiving and acknowledging subscriptions to the fund and keeping an accurate record of the sources from which the money came as each Company of the Volunteers was entitled to arms to the value of its subscriptions to the fund and the money collected by it. I don't know how this eventually worked out. Micheál O'Hanrahan was in charge of the fund from the time I lodged the money in the bank.[28]

One of the recipients of money from this fund was Seamus Daly who, with his brother Paddy, established a workshop for producing arms at the back of his family home. In January 1916, after a week or two of successfully making grenades and ammunition, Daly was asked to give up his job and devote his whole time to this work.

> This I did and a whole fortnight went by before there was any talk of payment in lieu of my normal earnings which, of course, were necessary to support a wife and three children. I saw Michael Staines who was then Assistant Brigade Quartermaster, and he told me to go and see Michael O'Hanrahan who used to work at Headquarters at No. 2, Dawson Street as a clerk. I never heard if he had a rank then, but I regarded him as a confidential secretary to the Headquarters Staff. I went to see O'Hanrahan and after waiting two hours he saw me and gave me thirty shillings and said my wages were to be 30/- a week. I reminded him that I had two weeks' wages coming to me. This surprised him. But I took the 30/- and thereafter I received this weekly wage.[29]

Again, Seamus Daly's Military Bureau evidence indicates that Miceál – along with his assistant Michael Staines – was the person with full responsibility for the supply and movement of weapons in the months before the Rising:

> About January 1916, I was speaking to someone at No. 2 Dawson Street, where I had been in connection with the distribution of the finished grenades. I think now it was Michael O'Hanrahan I was speaking to. He asked me if the

house, meaning 'Cluny', was still safe and advised us to keep as little stuff as possible on the premises and to get away as much of it as we could. I pointed out to him that we had to wait and get instructions from him or Michael Staines as to its disposal and he suggested I should see the Company Captain for the purpose of finding a place to dump the stuff in ... O'Hanrahan said there was grave danger at the moment, and they didn't know when the Government might strike. He told me to warn anyone who was helping us in the Munitions factory to be ready for a sudden order or instructions and whatever instructions we might get they were to be carried without question.[30]

Other activists remember Miceál Ua hAnnracáin as their authority for instruction as to what they should do with procured weapons. Aine Heron, a captain in Cumann na mBan, recalled being asked by Miceál to use her husband's shop in Phibsboro as a depot for ammunition.[31] After a robbery led by The O'Rahilly was carried out against Lawlor's hardware shop, Maire O'Brolchain was sent the stolen revolvers. These were collected by Miceál Ua hAnnracáin.[32]

Eily remembered that people came up from all over the country to obtain weapons from their house at 67 Connaught Street. Not all of them were dependable. After getting their arms from Connaught Street, issued to them by Dublin IRB member Seosamh Ua Ruairc, two Wexford Volunteers left the O'Hanrahan house with instructions to take a route that avoided the city centre. They ignored these orders, and their car promptly became stuck in a traffic jam at College Green, where Johnny Barton, one of the 'G' men, pulled it over on the basis of the Wexford registration. The shotguns and revolvers in the car were all seized and when news of this loss reached the O'Hanrahans, it left Eily and the rest of the family dreading a raid.[33]

Patrick Egan of the Fourth Battalion, in his statement for the Military Bureau, indicated the national scope of Miceál's work for the Volunteers.

> Michael O'Hanrahan was Quartermaster General. One day – I think it was in 1915 – he walked into our shop on the Quay. He asked me if I had the means of concealing some arms and ammunition, and if I was agreeable. I replied in the affirmative, and showed him over the premises. Shortly afterwards I received about fifty .32 Webley and Scott automatic revolvers and a large quantity of .22 ammunition. I think these came through Cullen's, Carriers, of Pearse Street. Occasionally lads from the country would call in and ask to see me, and, on presenting a note from Michael, would be handed over the goods.[34]

Despite Patrick Egan's clear statement that Miceál was Quartermaster General, there was some ambiguity over his rank. For example, when Michael Walker listed the officers in charge at Jacob's Biscuit Factory during the Rising, he wrote:

'Commandant Thomas McDonough, Michael O'Hanrahan, Major McBride, Commandant Thomas Hunter, Captain Dick McKee, Captain Slator, Capt. Colbert and Captain Meldon.' Careful as he was to give the men their full titles, it is clear that Walker did not know Miceál Ua hAnnracáin's exact position.[35]

In the 1930s a controversy developed as to who was the Quartermaster General of the Irish Volunteers in the run-up to the Easter Rising. Fine Gael, wanting to promote Michael Staines in the local election campaign of 1936, claimed in an issue of *United Ireland* that the 1916 Roll of Honour should have been presented to Staines, rather than Eamon de Valera, as the 'senior surviving officer of Easter Week' because Staines was 'Quartermaster General of the Irish Volunteers of all Ireland'.[36] This claim outraged Tomas Ua Raghallaigh, husband of Eily O'Hanrahan, who wrote to the *Irish Press* about this 'amazing assertion' and to state that the 'late Miceál O'Hanrahan, one of the sixteen executed leaders, was Quartermaster General of the Irish Volunteers'. He added, 'I have made definite detailed enquiries of most of the surviving Volunteer Officers of that period, including those who were in charge at Manchester, Liverpool and London and who were the actual intermediaries between the different Arms Companies and the QMG and they are positive and will verify on oath in any court that they furnished their reports, and were personally officially introduced to the late

Miceál O'Hanrahan as "The Quartermaster General".'[37]

When Michael Staines gave his 1949 statement to the Military Bureau, he claimed that he took up full-time duty as QMG on 16 March 1916, after a request to do so by Éamonn Ceannt (and again, he referred to himself as QMG in a further statement given to the Military Bureau in 1954).[38] There are two features of Staines's statement that do not easily fit with this claim: one is that he refers to the fact that up to the Rising he held the rank of captain, rather than commandant, the appropriate rank for the QMG. The other is that in his entire account of his various activities in regard to the duties of quartermaster – obtaining guns and ammunition, equipment, etc. – Staines never once mentions Miceál Ua hAnnracáin. Given that they worked closely together in similar roles, this is a peculiar omission and one consistent with a desire by Staines to avoid clarifying his relationship to Miceál.

In 1927, a note on a file to the pensions board also rated Miceál Ua hAnnracáin as captain, but this was on the basis only of his having been a battalion quartermaster (rather than QMG). Also, the adjudicators were well aware that the applicant, Eily, was an anti-Treaty republican, and they were in no humour to assist her in obtaining a full pension. In fact, as Countess Markievicz referred to him during the Rising and as the *Irish Press* wrote about him in later years, the role of Brigade Quartermaster, to whom everyone involved in the supply of arms was subordinate, meant that Miceál was effectively a commandant. Testimony from Seamus Daly confirms that the line of responsibility ran upwards from Michael Staines to Miceál Ua hAnnracáin. Even at the time there might have been tension over this point, but Daly makes it absolutely clear in his Military Bureau statement that Staines was the 'Assistant' Brigade Quartermaster:

Just before St Patrick's Day, 1916, I got an urgent message to prepare a parcel of grenades and a parcel of shot gun bayonets, and these were to be delivered to No. 2, Dawson Street by 9 o'clock that night. This was on a Thursday evening. Knowing that there were two other parties coming to the house that night for 'stuff' and it being my Company meeting night which I wanted to attend, I decided to ask the Company Captain to give me a reliable man to deliver the parcels in Dawson Street. I had brought the two parcels with me from 'Cluny' to Father Mathew Park. I asked Frank Henderson and he told me to pick a man. So I took Billy McGinley, a member of the Company, and told him I was sending him on a very important job. I advised him to walk and to go by the back streets as far as possible and not to talk to anyone on his way. I told him when he got to No. 2 Dawson Street to ask for Assistant Brigade Quartermaster Staines, and deliver to him the two parcels. On receiving my instructions, Billy went out but was back again almost immediately with a request to me to repeat the name of

the title of the man he was going to meet. I repeated the
words 'Assistant Brigade Quartermaster Staines', and Billy
ticked each word off on his fingers with the remark 'I hope
I won't forget these as some of these bloody fellows are very
particular about their titles'.[39]

Naturally, the role of quietly organising for the theft or
purchase of weapons and ensuring their most effective distribution to the Volunteers was not one that could be carried
out openly, but it is clear from the interviews conducted for
the Military Bureau and cited here that Miceál Ua hAnnracáin was quartermaster in charge of the procurement of
weapons and had a free hand in discharging this duty.

Inevitably, Miceál relied heavily upon the discretion of his
brother to assist with the task. Liam Tannam remembered
how 'Henry O'Hanrahan asked me could we get any buck
shot, five or six pellets, to fit into a 12 bore cartridge. He gave
me a mould which turned out about 20 at a time and I had
to pinch lead piping and my mother ran the moulds every
night. I brought the buck shot to No. 2 Dawson Street and
handed it over to Henry O'Hanrahan.'[40]

Another important financial responsibility for Miceál Ua
hAnnracáin came with the creation of an insurance fund
designed to assist those who might be sacked from their jobs
for participating in the Volunteers. In this project, Miceál
could draw upon the expertise of his brother Harry. John
MacDonagh recalled the project for the Military Bureau:

A society to insure Irish Volunteers against loss of their live-
lihood on account of their activities in the Volunteer movement was started at some stage. The O'Rahilly, Dr Conn
Murphy and I were appointed as a committee to administer
it, and I seem to remember that Micheál Ó Hannracháin
was the official but I can't say whether he was paid for it.
We used meet in O'Rahilly's house in Herbert Park occa-
sionally but as far as I remember the project fell through,
or perhaps the preparations for the Rising put an end to
it. I still have a copy of the Rules of the proposed Society,
which was called An Cumann Cosanta.[41]

The O'Hanrahans were also involved at a Dublin county
level in the planning of outings and social functions. Again,
these planning meetings were held in 2 Dawson Street.[42]
Miceál Ua hAnnracáin seems to have additionally held some
responsibility for appointments to the staff of the Irish Volunteers; it was he who informed TJ Meldon of his appointment
as Lieutenant to Headquarters Company, Fourth Battalion.
As well as these responsibilities, Miceál Ua hAnnracáin was
in charge of the weapons that found their way to Dublin
from Birmingham and London.[43]

During this time, Miceál studied intensely the subject
of military affairs and later, when it was thought necessary
to clear the house of potentially incriminating materials,
it took some effort to remove his large and heavy collection of military training books from 67 Connaught Street.[44]

He did not neglect fieldwork either and was keen that 'D' Company, Second Battalion, where he remained an officer, could use its weapons to the best of its ability. New Ross labourer Joseph McCarthy recalled a Sunday when two rival companies of Volunteers met for a competition in a village in the Dublin Mountains (after an afternoon of strenuous movements). 'A group of officers, including Eamon de Valera, Thomas MacDonagh, Michael O'Hanrahan and others were chatting about the day's events. O'Hanrahan was not satisfied with the umpire's report and de Valera placed his hand on O'Hanrahan's shoulder and playfully remarked to him, "disconsolate Micheal", which ended the debate with a good-humoured smile from O'Hanrahan.'[45]

While the brothers were working in key roles for the Volunteers, Eily and Máire were officers in the Ard Craobh of Cumann na mBan, where from about the time of the Howth gun-running they participated in the schooling of that organisation in first aid, stretcher drill, ceremonial drill, physical drill and signaling.[46] Initially, after joining in 1914, Eily attended the meetings at the back of the Catholic Commercial Club in O'Connell Street, the owners being under the impression that the women were working for England as part of the Red Cross.[47] After the Volunteers split, the same question of loyalty to John Redmond or Eoin MacNeill divided Cumann na mBan. Although Eily and the other women supporting MacNeill were in a majority, the nature of their organisation was discovered by the managers of the CCC and they lost their meeting room. The central branch of Cumann na mBan then moved to the hall at the back of 25 Parnell Square, where dances, céilithe and concerts were held to raise funds for the purchase of rifles for the Volunteers.[48]

The types of depot used for the concealment of arms around the city varied according to circumstance. Naturally, 67 Connaught Street had its complement of weapons carefully hidden about the premises. Another important depot was Joe McGuinness's drapery at 27 Dorset Street, where supplies of small arms and ammunition were delivered from England (and sometimes from Belfast) in cases with drapery goods. 'The cases would be opened usually in the evenings when the shop would be shut, and put into drapery parcels and paced in open racks. At times Mr McGuinness would be assisted by Peadar Clancy, Tom Hunter, Mícheál Staines, Mícheál O'Hanrahan and others.'[49]

The duties of the quartermaster involved a great deal more than the supply of weapons. As an editorial in *The Irish Volunteer* of 25 March 1916 explained:

The ideal Q.M. will have reserve stores of arms, ammunition, bandages, stretchers, splints, iodine, sacks, tools, utensils, lanterns, scaling ladders, gun-oil, pull-throughs. He will know how to estimate the food requirements of a squad, company, or battalion; the time to allow for making fires, cooking and eating; how to billet men in houses, stables, lofts; how to kill and cook fowl, pigs, sheep and beasts. The Q.M. who is not an expert in these matters should get busy instantly, or his men will slay him when the time for action comes. Moreover, he will have all supplies of food and useful stores in his district scheduled and be prepared to seize what he requires at a moment's notice; not forgetting the necessary horses, asses, carts, motors, etc., needed for transport.

In order to equip the Irish Volunteers in such a fashion and prepare the army for the Rising, Miceál Ua hAnnracáin worked behind the scenes with extraordinary dedication from 1913 to 1916. From his office work, his novel and his journalism, Miceál obtained an income of about £4 a week – considerably more than that of a skilled worker – of which he gave Mary £3 a week in upkeep.[50]

Chapter 8

1916

The Fighter

At least two months before the Rising, the date for the attempted insurrection was agreed upon and Miceál Ua hAnnracáin was one of the very few people outside of the Military Council of the IRB to know this. Sometime around February 1916, TJ Meldon recalled being asked by Miceál at Headquarters whether he could keep a secret. 'I said to him if he didn't think I could, he was not to tell me. He then informed me that a rising was about to take place and that I was to hand over my rifles as he said that staff officers would not require them.'[1]

With a month to go to the insurrection, the headquarters of the Irish Volunteers was put under permanent armed guard, so that in the event of a raid by members of 'G' Division, there would be sufficient time for critical papers to be destroyed.[2] This was particularly necessary because the plans for the Rising were kept in a safe at Dawson Street, while police scrutiny of the building was becoming more intense.[3] A week before the armed guards were stationed at Headquarters, the staff had discovered that people leaving the building were being shadowed. Robert Holland, an IRB and Fianna Éireann member, for example, reported being followed by a lady as far as James's Street Fountain, where he gave her the slip.[4]

The headquarters of the Volunteers also suffered from the anonymous destruction of a plate glass window in the large front office, the repair of which the building's owners, via Stanuell & Son, attempted to insist upon before the lease expired on the premises.[5] Rumours of an impending raid on 2 Dawson Street got the O'Hanrahans up one morning, when Seamus O'Connor knocked at 67 Connaught Street 'in a terrible state of excitement'. Suggesting to Eily that she mobilise a number of Cumann na mBan members, Miceál rushed down to Dawson Street. When the women arrived he had prepared papers for Eily to burn in the fire. Each of the women was then packed up with arms and ammunition and sent out under the noses of the detectives. At about ten o'clock that day, Bulmer Hobson arrived and looked round at all the commotion and the burning of papers. It seemed to an unimpressed Eily that he was indifferent to an imminent raid. Eily herself had a huge parcel to take from the building, which she brought to Joe McGuinness's drapery in Dorset Street.[6]

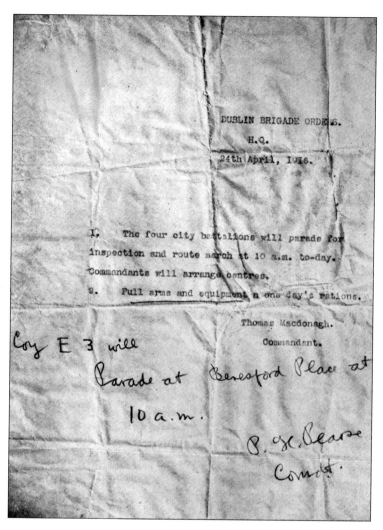

A mobilisation order for the Dublin brigades
authored by Michael's commandant, Thomas
MacDonagh, and Patrick Pearse on 24 April.

Right: Thomas MacDonagh was the Commandant of the Second Battalion of the Irish Volunteers in Jacob's Biscuit Factory during Easter Week.

Left: O'Hanrahan was to be second in command in Jacob's, but his duties were largely taken over by Major John MacBride, a veteran of the Second Boer War.

Above: An armoured car hastily assembled on behalf of the British, in the Inchicore Railworks, constructed using locomotive boilers.

Below: British soldiers form a barricade to hold off the Army of the Irish Republic during Easter Week.

Irish Rebellion – May 1916.
Holding a Dublin street against the Rebels.

In order to prevent the further slaughter of Dublin
citizens, and in the hope of saving the lives of our
followers now surrounded and hopelessly outnumbered, the
members of the Provisional Government present at Head-
Quarters have agreed to an unconditional surrender, and the
Commandants of the various districts in the City and Country
will order their commands to lay down arms.

P. H. Pearse
29th April 1916
3.45 p.m.

I agree to these conditions for the men only
under my own command in the Moore
Street District and for the men in
the Stephen's Green Command.

James Connolly
April 29/16

On consultation with Commandant Ceannt
and other officers I have decided to
agree to unconditional surrender also.

Thomas MacDonagh.

When Patrick Pearse's surrender
order (above) came through to
the Jacob's Garrison on 29 April,
Thomas Hunter (left) was one of
those who wished to keep fighting.

Above: Two republican prisoners are marched under British military escort to Kilmainham Jail.

Below: The yard at Kilmainham where the executions took place.

Above: An imagined scene of the executions at Kilmainham.

Right: Father Augustine Hayden, who gave the last rites to Michael.

IRISH REBELLION, MAY 1916

MICHAEL O'HANRAHAN
(Author of " The Swordsman of the Brigade," etc.),
Executed in Kilmainham Prison, May 4th, 1916.

Michael O'Hanrahan in memoriam.

I gCuimne Micil Uí Annracáin
do rugaḋ i Ros Mic Treoin 17·3·1877
do Lámacaḋ (le ḋlí Sasana)
i mBaile Áṫa Cliaṫ 4-5-1916.
An Céad Cat bríogáid Loc Garman
Teas d'Arm Poblacta
na h-Éireann do Tóg

IN MEMORY OF
MICHAEL O'HANRAHAN
BORN NEW ROSS 17-3-1877.
EXECUTED DUBLIN 4-5-1916.
ERECTED BY THE 1st BATTALION
SOUTH WEXFORD BRIGADE I.R.A.

TO THE MEMORY
OF
MICÉAL O'HANRAHAN.
FOUNDER MEMBER OF THIS CLUB.
Q.M.C. IRISH VOLUNTEERS 1916.
ONE OF THE EXECUTED LEADERS
OF THE RISING.

A ḊIA SAOR ÉIRE.

Two plaques dedicated to the memory of Michael O'Hanrahan in New Ross (above) and Carlow (left). The one above lists the date of his birth as St Patrick's Day 1877; on his birth certificate it is given as 16 January 1877.

The week before the Rising was an intense and hectic one for Miceál: a significant quantity of arms had to be moved about Dublin in the last few days before the insurrection and vital documents had to be removed from Headquarters. Gregory Murphy, member of IV Battalion and the IRB, remembered spending 'Holy Week with Con Donovan clearing depots and distributing arms, ammunition and explosives. I had a depot in my brother's shop in Rathmines – a cycle shop where the Post Office is now situated and in my own home in Carnew Street – I helped Michael O'Hanrahan to move a case of revolvers from Seamus O'Connor's house in Woodville Terrace, Drumcondra.'[7]

On Sunday 16 April, after his usual parade with 'D' Company, Second Battalion, Miceál Ua hAnnracáin fell in with Seumas Kavanagh (who later, after 1917, would become captain of 'H' Company, Fourth Battalion) on their way home. Kavanagh responded willingly to Miceál's request that he join Headquarters staff with a particular responsibility:

[Miceál Ua hAnnracáin] informed me that a man would call, probably the following morning, in a taxi, giving me a description of the man, and that his name would be Eamon Tierney. He would be tall, thin and dark, with a strong English accent and would wear a 'G.R.' band on his arm, indicating that he was a member of the British Home Guard. He would have a number of suitcases with him containing small arms and ammunition. I was to receive him and take the cases from him, see that he was fed and rested and back on the mailboat that evening. This was to take place several times during the week. And on placing the arms and ammunition away safely I was to inform Mícheál O'Hanrahan as to their arrival. At this time Mícheál O'Hanrahan lived in Connaught Street. During the week both he and his brother Harry would call to remove some of the arms. This happened repeatedly during the week.[8]

On the Wednesday before Easter Sunday, Miceál told Eily to meet with himself, Thomas MacDonagh and Seán MacDiarmada at 25 Parnell Square. On her arrival there at 8.30pm, the three men were standing at the foot of the stairs and they gave Eily a dispatch for Enniscorthy, saying only that it was very important that it reach the leader of the Volunteers in that town. It seemed odd to Eily that no one gave her a name, and she later speculated that perhaps a split at Headquarters meant that there was uncertainty about the issue among those planning the Rising. It was late when Miceál came home that night and Eily was already asleep. But early in the morning she went to Miceál's room and asked, 'Can you tell me to whom to deliver it?'

'I suggest you go to the *Echo* office and ask for Seamus Doyle. Don't give it to anyone else,' was Miceál's reply. At this point, Eily guessed that the Rising was at hand. That Miceál was very close to the Military Council of the IRB, who were planning the Rising, and that he was closely involved in its preparation, is shown by this incident and his actions over the next three days. Yet Miceál rarely spoke of the impending insurrection, not even intimating to Eily that it was under way.[9]

Either that same Wednesday evening or possibly on the Thursday night before the Rising, Miceál went looking for Kitty O'Doherty, the quartermaster of Cumann na mBan, who was not at her home further down Connaught Street. Together with the prominent IRB member Seamus O'Connor, Miceál then went to 25 Parnell Square where Cumann na mBan were holding a final meeting. 'What is it?' asked Kitty. Seamus O'Connor told her, hurriedly, about guns that were in O'Shea's house in Arran Road, Drumcondra. He said: 'You must get them. We want you to save them.'[10]

Throughout the week, many Volunteers were ordered to Dawson Street by their officers to collect weapons. William James Stapleton, for example, obtained a single-barrel shotgun and some ammunition from 2 Dawson Street.[11] It was more difficult, however, given the police scrutiny, to move larger amounts of weaponry, as Liam Tannam recalls.

On Holy Thursday I got a message from Barney Mellows to come to 2 Dawson Street. He told me he thought the police were on to a consignment of high-power .22 rifles, a couple of cases of them, which were in Volunteer Headquarters, and that he was anxious to remove them to a safe place. He had already got in touch with Jimmy Fitzgerald of Great Brunswick Street [now Pearse Street]. I arrived at 7. I was then armed with a .38 revolver. Barney Mellows, Jimmy Fitzgerald and I think, Seumas Cooling, were there. Hoey, the 'G' man, was standing on the opposite side of the street. Barney said, 'I wonder could we shift Hoey.'

I left the building and crossed the road, stood behind Hoey and coughed. He turned round quickly in surprise and as I continued to stand behind him, he apparently got a bit nervous and changed his position and moved down about ten yards. I followed him down and repeated the manoeuvre. When he turned I gave him a rather determined look and he left his position. A taxi came round the corner of Nassau Street, pulled up opposite No. 2 Dawson Street by arrangement. I don't know who the driver of the taxi was. We were ready in the hall with the cases and put them quickly into the taxi which they almost filled, we got in beside them and drove off and by a circuitous route eventually arrived at the back of Clarendon Street Church.[12]

From that Thursday, additional guards were summoned to Headquarters and given orders from Miceál Ua hAnnracáin to defend the building by force of arms if necessary.[13] During the evening of Holy Thursday, Miceál returned home to talk to Charlie Monahan and Con Keating, who were at 67 Connaught Street before they started on their journey to Kerry.

Monahan and Keating were to dismantle a radio transmitter in Kerry and contact the *Aud*, the ship with the arms for the Rising that Roger Casement had obtained through negotiations with the German government. The men were then expected to assist with the distribution of her 20,000 rifles, ten machine guns, and a million rounds of ammunition. Intercepted by three British sloops, the loss of the *Aud* and those arms was a catastrophe for those who had staked the possibility of success in the Rising on the German weapons. It was also a personal tragedy for Monahan and Keating (along with Donal Sheehan of Newcastlewest), who drowned when their car went over the pier wall at Ballykissane. Eily O'Hanrahan, who had returned from Enniscorthy earlier in the day, remembered that Miceál had never been so deeply affected as he was over the news of this accident.[14]

Eily recalled: 'On Friday and Saturday things were boiling. Miceál was hurrying here and there. We were busy giving out arms and equipment and foodstuffs to the Volunteers.'[15] Miceál spent most of Friday at Headquarters, which naturally was the focus for a great deal of activity. There was a large contingent from Cumann na mBan in the building all day, making field dressings for the Volunteers.[16] It was necessary to bring in the last of the workshop arms and have them distributed, as well as to make various other last-minute arrangements. For example, Gearoid Ua h-Uallachain met Seán MacDiarmada at Headquarters at 3pm to deliver some bayonets he had in his possession and bring six automatic pistols to a house in Palmerstown Place, near Broadstone.[17] There, Gearoid borrowed a green bicycle from Michael Malone, who was on duty at Headquarters that night and would soon be killed in the most intense fighting of the Rising at Mount Street Bridge.[18]

At this point, Eoin MacNeill, the chief of staff of the Irish Volunteers, was prevaricating over whether to approve of a Rising on the Sunday. The previous night, Patrick Pearse, Thomas MacDonagh and Seán MacDiarmada had persuaded MacNeill that with the weapons from the *Aud*, the Rising could have a serious chance of success. Moreover, wasn't it better to fight than to be suppressed without resistance? After all, a document had been read into the record of Dublin Corporation on the Wednesday, purporting to show British plans for an imminent crackdown against the Volunteers.

Early on Good Friday, MacNeill ordered Miceál Ua hAnnracáin to contact Kitty O'Doherty, to ask her to meet him at Headquarters with some trusted messengers. Miceál arrived at 32 Connaught Street, where Kitty lived, just before 10am. Having received his news, Kitty hurried down to Dawson Street, where she found ...

    ... confusion at headquarters. Barney Mellows was singing. The women of the Cumann na mBan were taking out the remainder of the stuff. They were in a room on the right-hand side of the front. Eoin MacNeill and Barney Mellows were in a room on the left-hand side of the first floor. I went straight to Eoin MacNeill. His face was a study to me. He was always very sallow. He now had two huge pink spots. He said to me: 'I want you.' He did not ask me about the messengers. He said: 'Wait a while. I want to give you all my private papers.'[19]

In other words, whether convinced or not, MacNeill was preparing for the Rising and the likelihood of a raid on 2 Dawson Street.

The previous day a party of eight people, with twelve trunks containing arms, left London and arrived in Dublin on the Friday morning, to report to Headquarters. Miceál was very disappointed with the delivery, however, expressing his disgust and saying that he wished they had brought more ammunition than revolvers, as that was the pressing need.[20]

Eamon Tierney, who had also been bringing arms in from London, realised that a Rising was being prepared for the near future and told Seumas Kavanagh, his contact in Dublin, that he intended to stay and join the fight. This was reported to Miceál on Friday, who remarked, 'Well, we can't deprive him, having done so much, of taking part in the fight.' Tierney gave a good account of himself in Church Street during the rebellion and survived the Rising unharmed.[21]

Also on the Friday before the Rising, Miceál ordered purchases of the various types of equipment that were available in shops – canteens, webbing, socks, bandoliers, green collars, hats, etc. – from Lawlor's of Fownes Street, Fallon's of Mary Street, and PJ Bourke's of North Frederick Street. Much of this was brought to 67 Connaught Street, where a meeting was held on the Friday evening to arrange for the distribution of the arms and ammunition. The three O'Hanrahan sisters agreed to stay at the house to hand out the remaining equipment.[22]

After the meeting, at about 7pm, Miceál went to see IRB member Leo Henderson at his house adjacent to Father Mathew Park to brief him on the forthcoming Rising. There he met Leo's brother, Frank, whom he knew very well. As Miceál was leaving Frank asked, 'Well, Miceál, are we going out on Sunday and not coming back again?' Miceál trusted Frank sufficiently to reply, 'Yes, we are going out, and not coming back.'[23]

Around this time, Miceál also called into the house of Martin and Peg Conlon, 36 Cabra Park, to ask could Peg stand ready to take a message to Wexford whenever it was needed.[24] Despite such preparations and a general air among the Volunteers that the Rising was imminent, the necessary preparatory work was carried out in great secrecy. So when, on the Saturday, IRB member Peadar Mac Cana from the Irish Volunteer Battalion, Newry, came from Newry to Headquarters for information 'and made inquiries in guarded terms of the young woman in charge there', he was told 'that nothing unusual had happened or was about to happen'.[25]

Another visitor to Headquarters on Easter Saturday was

Seamus Daly, who had been running the Irish Volunteers' main workshop. Seamus was allowed to see Miceál: 'I asked him how were things. He asked me how were things in the Workshop. I said that everything was practically cleared out now, that we delivered all the stuff, and was there any use in carrying on with any more work, and he said: "I don't think there will be any time to" and then he said: "as a matter of fact, we may be in the field any time now. Expect anything that happens." And then he said: "Keep in touch with your Company, and wait for any orders."'[26]

A rather more tricky visitor to deal with was a young woman named Cregan, who had arranged to meet Bulmer Hobson at 2 Dawson Street to spend Easter with him on a romantic trip to the north. At this time, Hobson was under house arrest at 76 Cabra Park for fear that he would realise that the Rising was imminent and sabotage it. So 'Máire', as Seamus Ua Caomhanaigh recalled (probably misremembering her name, since Claire Cregan was Hobson's fiancée and future wife)[27], spent the day ...

> ... wondering where he was and what was delaying him. Barney Mellows would tell her he'd gone out for a bit and would soon be back. As the day wore on she became more and more perturbed. I don't know what eventually happened as I left the office before she did, but it became common knowledge afterwards why he didn't turn up to meet her on that day. I was told afterwards that the police

spent a lot of time digging holes looking for him and thinking something worse happened to him than what had.[28]

During Easter Saturday, 22 April 1916, Eoin MacNeill
learned that the shipment of German arms had been lost.
That night, deciding to halt an insurrection that he no longer
felt was justified, MacNeill convened a meeting of his supporters and began to draft his 'countermanding order'. On
discovering this, the advocates of a rising met to discuss their
options. Thus, around midnight, two Dublin bodies were
attempting to put their very opposite stamps on the situation: MacNeill's ad hoc committee (which included figures
like Seán T O'Kelly, Arthur Griffith and The O'Rahilly) and
the Military Council of the IRB.

The result, inevitably, was horrible confusion.

After sending orders all over the country to instruct the
Volunteers not to take any action on the Sunday, in the
early hours of the morning of Sunday 23 April, MacNeill
cycled to the *Sunday Independent* offices in person and
inserted the notice rescinding all orders for mobilisations
later in the day. Once the newspapers hit the streets, the
Military Council gathered again to assess how best to cope
with this crisis. Those Volunteers like Miceál Ua hAnnracáin who knew that the Rising was due to start later that
day but who were not members of the Military Council of
the IRB, were left in a high state of nervousness and anxi-
ety. As Kitty O'Doherty recalled:

Sunday nobody knew what was happening. People
kept coming in and out and talking excitedly. Michael
O'Hanrahan came [to 32 Connaught Street]. Liam Archer,
Diarmuid Hegarty, Fionan Lynch, Paddy Moran, Michael
Staines and Gearoid O'Sullivan came in the evening and I
remember giving them all rashers and eggs. During Sunday,
in spite of the countermanding order in the paper, I myself
received a mobilisation order. This was contradicted later.
The men were discussing the same thing. Their mobilisation orders were cancelled and they were to stand to.[29]

Richard Hayes, future TD and film censor, had a similar
experience of the muddled situation. Having mobilised his
men, Hayes came down from Rathbeale Cross, a few miles
north of Swords, to seek clarification and got none.

The evening passed and night came, but no order arrived.
A little after midnight Frank Lawless and myself drove to
Dublin. We called at several prominent and friendly houses
but could get no response to knocking and bellringing. At
last we were admitted to a house in North Richmond Street
where we found Michael O'Hanrahan and Tom Weafer
(the former executed, the latter killed in the Rising). They
seemed as confused as ourselves, telling us that things were
postponed and that the best thing to do would probably be
to disband the men who, however, were to be informed that
they could expect to be mobilised at any moment.[30]

Late on the Sunday, the situation was resolved with the Military Council determined to go ahead, despite the combined blows of the loss of the weapons on the *Aud* and the countermanding order. After midnight a meeting was underway at 67 Connaught Street with Miceál, Harry, Eamonn Price, Dick Cotter, Peadar MacMahon, the Meldons and others. A knock on the door brought them all to their feet, ready to fire if there was a raid, but it was Diarmuid O'Hegarty with orders for Eily to bring to Enniscorthy on the Monday and for Máire Lawless to bring to Swords.[31]

On Easter Monday, 24 April 1916, Miceál Ua hAnnracáin got up early and marched with his battalion to St Stephen's Green. Once there he set up the staff office at Number 130 on the west side of the square, at a small tobacconist shop beside May's music shop where the poet and actor Blanaid Salkeld had placed a first-floor room at the disposal of Thomas MacDonagh. With Miceál at the staff office were Adjutant Tom Slater, Tom Hunter – acting commandant – and somewhat late, as his mobilisation orders to personally report to Miceál had earlier missed him, Seumas Kavanagh.[32]

On his arrival, Seumas Kavanagh was ordered to take a cab to go to the depots on Sherrard Street and the O'Hanrahan house on Connaught Street to collect all remaining arms and ammunition. Kavanagh suggested commandeering a motor car, but Miceál said that such an action was likely to cause a commotion and a cab would be less suspicious.[33] Returning to the park, Kavanagh unloaded the cab on orders of Countess Markievicz, who explained that the weapons were needed at her position on the Green (where she was second-in-command to Michael Mallin), but that she would have 'Commandant' O'Hanrahan notified.[34] Into another cab, maps, proclamations and some home-made grenades were gathered from TJ Meldon's office but, fearing interception, the vehicle was directed to the GPO rather than Jacob's.[35]

Shortly after twelve on Monday, a group of 150 men under the command of Thomas MacDonagh, many from Miceál's Second Battalion, broke into Jacob's Biscuit Factory on the Bishop Street side. The keys that had been secured for the purpose did not work and so entry was made through a window about six feet from the ground. This was to be the main route in and out of the position. Six policemen who had been attracted to this activity were arrested and remained prisoners of the Volunteers until their release on the Sunday.[36]

Jacob's was a very large employer, with over 3,000 men and women in the workforce, many of whom were local residents. Having planned the occupation in advance, the rebels moved quickly through the building, securing it and obliging the skeleton staff of bank holiday workers to leave (with the exception of the caretaker, who insisted on staying).[37] Among the occupying force was Miceál Ua hAnnracáin. It was logical that the quartermaster for the insurrection should be stationed at the premises that acted as the main source of food supply for the participants of the Rising.

In Jacob's, Miceál's duties as second-in-command were largely taken over by Major John MacBride, who had volunteered to assist the rebels when, while walking through St Stephen's Green, he saw Thomas MacDonagh in uniform and offered his services. The addition of MacBride to the officer staff of the Volunteers in Jacob's was fortuitous, because Miceál suffered an injury that undermined his ability to play a full role in events. Shortly after the factory had been occupied, while making himself familiar with the interior of what was a very large building, Miceál walked down a pitch-dark passage, where he unexpectedly encountered a steep stone stairway and fell heavily in the darkness, striking his head on the stone and stunning himself. Thereafter, he had no appetite and was dazed and appeared in pain. He asked those who knew of the accident to say nothing to MacDonagh or MacBride, for fear he would be sent to hospital. Almost certainly, though, he was suffering from concussion.[38]

By Tuesday morning, Miceál was recovered enough that he could disguise his injury from his sister Eily. They met when, having returned from Enniscorthy and reported to the GPO, Eily went to Jacob's where she urged the men inside to lower a ladder for her, a risky business due to sniper fire from British soldiers. When they saw this, a crowd of hostile residents began to gather and insult her. Eily's entrance was held up for some time, with a sceptical John MacBride having to be assured that she was Miceál's sister before she was let inside. There, she reported to MacDonagh and Miceál and asked permission to stay and assist the Jacob's garrison. Miceál and MacDonagh instead ordered Eily to return to 67 Connaught Street to distribute equipment to those who sought it, then to get rid of everything in anticipation of a raid on the house.[39] MacDonagh also had a message for Patrick Pearse: that he needed grenades and that MacBride had been commissioned. As Eily was seen off by Miceál, tears came to the eyes of brother and sister. MacDonagh reassured Eily that she would see Miceál again, a statement which proved to be true but only to the extent that Eily had a few minutes with her brother at Kilmainham Jail the night before his execution.[40]

That Miceál paid attention to the role of every individual as well as the movement as a whole is shown by an exchange he had with Eily during her visit to Jacob's. While Eily was present, Miceál took the opportunity to ask her about a Volunteer, Seamus O'Doherty, who had been doubtful of the value of a rising. Miceál asked Eily whether O'Doherty was out and she – at random – replied 'yes, of course'. In fact, Miceál was right to be concerned as to whether O'Doherty had been pursuaded to fight, as O'Doherty left Dublin with his family on the Tuesday.[41]

Again, on leaving, Eily had to run the gauntlet of the hostile crowd. Among this body was a woman who gave the rebels 'considerable trouble with her abusive conduct'. Yet, as TJ Meldon recalled, after this woman received a slight injury from a splinter of stone and was taken to the Adelaide Hospital, 'she returned, a totally changed woman, whether it was from the sobering effects of the night's rest or the influence of one of the Church St priests, or both, and where there were curses before, blessings were now showered on us, during which time a messenger passing by with a basket of groceries and fruit halted, whereon she commandeered the contents, throwing them into the window, thus providing us with a welcome addition to our repast of plasmon biscuits.'[42] Clerical intervention certainly assisted the Volunteers with the hostile crowds around Jacob's: when the shouting from the mob outside was at its loudest, 'an old priest came along and before them all, made the sign of the Cross at all parts of the building. This acted like magic on the mob, and they melted away.'[43]

Earlier that Tuesday morning, the quartermaster's supplies for the men and women at Jacob's were augmented by the success of a raid in search of provisions. Intercepting two bread vans, which had just left their bakery, the rebels obtained 'a large quantity of milk, beef, mutton, bacon and many kinds of tinned food. This food was very welcome, for although Jacob's had stores of chocolate and crystalized fruit, such sweets soon sickened those who gorged on them. They also had a quantity of boots and the contents of McEvoy's stores on Redmond's Hill and Larkin's tobacco and chandlery stores, Wexford Street. On the same day, clergymen were admitted to hear confessions and absolve every man, as the rebels expected an attack any moment.'[44]

The initial cordon of British troops deployed around Dublin did not touch Jacob's, and on the Wednesday the Volunteers had to face only a certain amount of sniper fire. Throughout the day, the level of gunfire increased as the fighting intensified at the nearby College of Surgeons and at some of the factory outposts. It was still possible to travel through the city and it is claimed that Harry went to the GPO. According to the Military Bureau account of Patrick Rankin, a painter and IRB member from Newry, on the Wednesday at the GPO, 'Tom Clarke introduced me to Henry O'Hanrahan who was in charge of the rifles and ammunition, and he issued a Lee Enfield and ammunition to me. Never will I forget the kind features of Henry, he seemed so out of place in charge of such weapons, one could imagine him more at home in a library of books, but he had the heart of a lion which he proved in death.'[45] The reference to a brave death seems to suggest a confusion between Harry and Miceál. The description of a man in charge of weapons who would have looked more at home among books would fit either of the brothers, but in the absence of any other testimony that places Henry in the GPO, the likelihood is that Rankin was mistaken.

Moreover, Harry was in charge of the supply store and canteen at Jacob's, a post that kept him busy in the factory. This was a store that ...

> ... was plentifully provided with clothing, boots, tobacco and commodities that made for personal comfort displayed on long benches. The store was much appreciated, under-clothing, socks &c. were a boon to many, after three days almost of 24 hours continued activity in complete original attire, through which flour and grime had penetrated to cake in sweaty shirts without even removing our boots. The luxury of washing one's feet in a bucket, a new pair of socks, a pair of new boots and we felt we could march to the Wicklow hills and fight every inch of the way, if necessary.[46]

An enthusiastic and confident mood among the Volunteers and Cumann na mBan members at Jacob's was dampened, literally, on the Wednesday night. At 11pm the fire alarm of the factory was triggered, leading to a deluge from the sprinklers. Anxious for the supplies of flour in the factory, the caretaker urged the Volunteer officers to take action and thanks to the presence of a plumber among them, the water could be turned off.[47] That night, the sky was deep red from the fires that were raging in the city.

One issue to be addressed on the Thursday by a garrison

still – on the whole – in good cheer, was that of a flag for the position. Miceál and the other officers had forgotten to bring the tricolour that had been made in advance of the uprising, so with some green and white bunting and yellow grass cloth, a very fine flag was made and hoisted. Surviving even after the surrender of the garrison, this was the last of the rebel flags to fly over Dublin.[48]

In between organising raids and excursions and improving the defences of the factory, the Volunteers were given periods of rest time, and during these a study circle formed based on certain of the books taken from a small library in Jacob's. Seosamh de Brun, Second Battalion, recalled discussing quotes by Julius Caesar.[49] But news was coming in of battles elsewhere and of the deaths of friends and admired Volunteer leaders. Again and again, the value of the insurrection was discussed, and there was a great deal of speculation as to what the future would hold in the event of defeat. All the same, the Jacob's garrison clung to the hope that the country would rise and alongside a number of fanciful rumours came more accurate reports of heroic efforts being made to resist the British Army at Mount Street Bridge and at the South Dublin Union.[50]

On the Friday of the Rising, the Jacob's garrison was kept as busy as ever. As the major stores of food under rebel control were kept at the factory, the production of bread went on. But communication with other garrisons was almost impossible now that the British troops had such a large presence in the city centre. Learning of the battles around Mount Street, MacDonagh called for volunteers for a sortie. Twenty cyclists were formed up into a diversionary party to relieve the pressure on the Boland's Mill garrison there. This party had travelled only as far as Merrion Square when heavy fire forced them back and into more difficulties from British troops in Grafton Street and Leeson Street: but for covering fire from the Volunteers in the Shelbourne Hotel there would have been many more casualties than the one they did incur (John O'Grady, whose stomach was torn out of his body by a bullet; although his comrades got him back to Jacob's, he died shortly after being moved to the Adelaide Hospital).[51]

With the sudden drop in volume of gunfire on Saturday, Miceál and the rest of the men and women in Jacob's would have begun to fear the worst, fears that were realised on Sunday morning when two Capuchin friars, Fr Aloysius and Fr Augustine, came into the factory with Patrick Pearse's order to all the commandants to surrender to save the lives of their followers. MacDonagh, believing that an order from Pearse, then a prisoner, was not binding, went with the priests, under a flag of truce, to find out the facts of the position.[52] When he returned to the factory, he convened a meeting of his officers. They listened quietly and intently to his report. After explaining Pearse's order, MacDonagh made the point that they were nevertheless free to make their own decision. One by one, the officers gave their opinions.

A fervent speech was made by Séamus Hughes, who argued that surrender would mean giving the leaders over to the British to be killed by firing squad, and that rather than this, it were better to die, gun in hand, fighting to the last. Miceál spoke after Hughes and, despite the fact that he was one of those likely to face execution, in his 'slow, calmed and reasoned tone', he advocated surrender. To continue the fight was simply to invite the destruction of the factory by incendiary shells and not merely the factory but also the residences that crowded around Jacob's. Nor was escaping to the country in small groups a realistic alternative.[53]

With the majority of officers agreeing, MacDonagh summed up, with tears in his eyes and his voice breaking: 'Boys, we must give in. We must leave some to carry on the struggle.' Next the decision had to be told to the full garrison and it sparked a furious reaction, as Bob Price recalled. 'When the garrison was assembled on the ground floor there was a scene of incredible pandemonium and confusion. Men, old in the movement, seeing their dearest hopes dashed to the ground became hysterical weeping openly, breaking their rifles against the walls. Others took things more quietly but grimly prepared for the inevitable. I advised the very young lads and the older married men with dependent children who were not in uniform to try to get away. I must say that not all took that course but stuck manfully to their officers.'[54]

Again, Thomas Pugh also remembered that moment, as crying men smashed their rifles rather than let them fall into British hands. MacDonagh 'made a short sensible speech, he was very cool and very much to the point. Some of the lads asked MacBride what they should do, should they try to escape or should they remain there, and he said "Liberty is a sweet thing. If it ever happens again, take my advice and don't get inside four walls."'[55]

Another eyewitness to the scene was Seosamh de Brun:

Some one asked what would happen the Commandant and other Leaders. McDonagh replied that for himself he did not know but he was assured the lives of the men would be safe. Father Augustine here intervened and said he was present at the conference with General Maxwell and was assured the Army would be treated as prisoners of war.

There were loud cries of dissent amongst the men against surrender. Many were crying fiercely and shouting, 'Fight it out!' 'Fight it out!' 'We will fight it out!' Dick McKee was most vehemently opposed to surrender. Volunteer O'Malley – a Tailor by trade – loudly demanded to 'fight it out', brandishing his shotgun. The Senior Officers, Commandants McBride and Hunter, were silent. They were resigned to the inevitability of surrender. Some one said the garrison was to march out carrying their arms and flags as prisoners of war. I was with Commandant Hunter after the parade broke up. He also wept bitterly with disappointment at the end of the struggle. Many of the men smashed their guns on the steel floors rather than surrender them to the British. Numbers of the men were given the option to escape from the building and availed of it.[56]

Tom Hunter was one of those who argued against surrendering and in favour of a continuation of the fight, but MacBride answered that he thought there was no chance of success and added that 'we must now save the lives of our people'. This helped swing the debate.[57] It was indeed possible to save lives at this stage and in fact escape for those who wished it was a real possibility. Indeed, even after the Volunteers had marched out of the building to surrender, there was still an opportunity for some of the men and women to avoid imprisonment.

Padraig O'Kelly, Fourth Battalion, recalled that 'before we reached the British, some of the boys just walked out into the crowd which almost lined the way to the point of surrender, and escaped. The leaders who included Thomas MacDonagh, Major MacBride and Michael O'Hanrahan could as easily have escaped. However, they presumably thought they were in honour bound by their agreement to surrender, and "the hit and run" technique of the Black-and-Tan days had not been developed.'[58]

It is interesting to speculate on how their roles might have evolved had Miceál, MacDonagh and MacBride slipped into the crowds and gone on the run. But on that Sunday it would never have crossed their minds to do so, because at this stage what was uppermost in their thoughts was that by their bearing in the face of defeat and execution, they could assist the battle for the hearts and minds of the people of Ireland. As Miceál put it to Harry, a short time before his death, 'We may go under and have to suffer the penalty, but in my opinion Ireland is saved.'[59]

Filing up New Bride Street, the Volunteers walked proudly under the gaze of their officers, who stood to the side while all their arms were laid down via a series of parade-ground commands. Miceál and Harry availed of the opportunity to give their money (about £3) to Elizabeth O'Farrell, the nurse who had braved gunfire from British troops to carry the white flag that initiated the surrender. Two days after the death of Miceál, O'Farrell called up to Connaught Street and handed over the money.[60]

MacDonagh, MacBride and Miceál Ua hAnnracáin took their places at the head of the troops as – with cordons of British soldiers to the front, sides and rear – the prisoners moved off towards Richmond Barracks, the doctors and nurses of the Adelaide Hospital gazing solemnly out of their windows as they passed.[61]

Chapter 9

30 April to 4 May 1916

The Prisoner

When the Volunteers from Jacob's garrison reached Bull Alley Road, they found Éamonn Ceannt and his men lined up to meet them. There the British told the men to discard all military equipment. To discourage the civilians who were watching proceedings from their houses, the British soldiers pretended to fire at the windows and shouted at the residents to close them. It was late afternoon by the time the body of Volunteers – now some four hundred strong – arrived at Richmond Barracks, and they were met by an angry crowd, mostly the wives of soldiers who were serving in the British Army. Once inside, everyone was gathered in a cold barrack room, which felt crowded given the large numbers being held. Thomas Pugh remembered seeing MacDonagh take off his big military cloak to give it to MacBride.[1]

There were no beds in the room; nothing except a few

blankets, insufficient to cover all those being held captive. A large iron tub in one corner provided the only latrine facilities available to the occupants. Nor was there any food. The following morning, Monday 1 May, everyone was marched around the barrack square for a half an hour to an hour, before being shoved back into a different barrack room, starving. The officers from Jacob's, however, including MacDonagh, MacBride, Miceál and Harry, were separated from their men and brought to a gymnasium where a selection process was taking place.[2]

Joseph Lawless, Irish Volunteers Fingal, recalled being brought into that room, where life-and-death decisions were being made:

Later on that day [Monday 1 May], we were all marched across to the gymnasium where we were lined up against the wall on the right-hand side. Over against the wall on the left-hand side were about twenty prisoners, amongst whom I recognised Sean McDermott, Eamon Ceannt, Sean Heuston, Willie Pearse, Michael O'Hanrahan, Con Colbert, Tom Clarke, John McBride and Thomas McDonagh.

Michael O'Hanrahan, McDermott and one or two others were sitting on the floor with their backs to the wall, and the others leaned against the wall, except Ceannt, who strode up and down in front of them with arms folded, looking very much like a caged lion. Sean McDermott and Colbert smiled and nodded cheerily across to each one of us in turn, but it was clear to us then, that these men across the room had been selected from the general body of prisoners, and that the purpose of our entry to this building was for similar selection. This estimate was confirmed within a few minutes when a military officer conducted two or three R.I.C. sergeants towards us, who proceeded to walk slowly up and down in front of us, carefully scrutinising each one from head to foot. Then there was a consultation between them and the military officers present, and Tom Ashe, Dr Hayes, Frank Lawless and Jim Lawless were picked out and ordered across the room to join the select band on the other side, while the rest of us were marched back to our original barrack room.[3]

Directing the selection process that had seen Miceál and Harry separated from their battalion, to be put among those facing execution, were the senior political detectives of the Dublin Metropolitan Police. Immediately after the surrender these detectives had gone to Richmond Barracks to identify the best-known Volunteer leaders for immediate court-martial. It was here that Miceál's hard work from 2 Dawson Street – as recorded in the political record books of the detectives – counted against him. Eamon Broy, the famous rebel sympathiser within the DMP, explains:

It was then that the political record books in the Detective Office were brought into use. The books were taken to [Dublin] Castle and, I believe, subsequently to Richmond Barracks.

The records might show, for example, that Michael O'Hanrahan met Thomas McDonagh in Grafton St. three months before and had a conversation of some minutes duration. That did not appear to be an important item to be recorded but, when it was brought forward at the trial of O'Hanrahan, it was an additional proof, apart from his participation in the Rising, of his general anti-British activities. The record books consequently assumed a more sinister role than one would have thought reading them before Easter Week, 1916.[4]

A sentry was on duty, walking up and down to keep those on the left separated from the rest of the Volunteers.[5] The business of sorting the prisoners took all day Tuesday and at a very late hour (1.25am, Wednesday 3 May 1916) those selected by the detectives were led from the room. Ten to fifteen minutes later, having heard the charge against him, Miceál returned to the gymnasium.[6]

At this moment, General John Maxwell, who had been sent to Dublin to deal with the Rising and was effectively the ruler of Ireland thanks to the Defence of the Realm Act and a Royal Proclamation, was planning to execute some seventy-five men and women. The wide range of potential victims he had in mind is shown by his letter to Lord John French, Commander of the British Home Forces, on 4 May 1916, in which he wrote in an irritated tone that Eoin MacNeill's life would probably be lobbied for by priests and politicians:

'I am a little perplexed what to do about this man McNeill, he is no doubt one of the most prominent in the movement though I believe he did try and stop the actual rebellion taking place when it did. The Priests and politicians will try and save him – He is not tried yet.'[7] Maxwell was also keen to have Countess Markievicz shot, but intervention by Prime Minister Asquith prevented his sentence from being carried out.[8]

A series of hurried court-martial hearings had begun with those of Patrick Pearse, Thomas MacDonagh and Tom Clarke on the Tuesday evening, leading to their executions around dawn the following day, 3 May. That day too, it was Miceál's turn for his court-martial. As with all the proceedings, no member of the press or public was allowed to attend. The president of the court was Brigadier-General Charles Blackader and Miceál was tried under the name of 'Michael O'Haurehan'. The only witness brought to give evidence against Miceál was Major JA Armstrong, who testified that Miceál was an officer and had been in a party of men who had fired shots in the vicinity of Jacob's, causing several casualties. Armstrong also claimed that as an officer, Miceál was armed, but this assertion had to be withdrawn after Miceál challenged him. For his defence, Miceál simply said, 'As a soldier of the Republican army acting under orders of the Provisional Government of that Republic duly constituted I acted under the orders of my superiors.'[9]

This statement was formulated without Miceál knowing what approach to the courts-martial his co-accused would take. The words he chose were simultaneously a brief, straightforward, soldierly response to the accusation – a response that would be respected by his comrades – and one that (worth a try under the circumstances) would leave open the possibility that the authorities might not number him among the ringleaders. Miceál's statement was true; it asserted the legitimacy of the cause for which he had fought, namely the Provisional Government of the Republic; and it hid the level of his involvement in the preparations for the Rising. In the unlikely event that the authorities were unsure about Miceál's seniority, he was not going to voluntarily say anything that would confirm that they had captured someone who had a major organisational role in the rebellion.

The other Volunteer officers faced with the same question – what response should they give to their interrogators? – took a range of positions from outright defiance (perhaps most dramatically in the case of Willie Pearse's 'guilty' statement) to non-recognition of the court (James Connolly) to serious attempts to mount a defence and deny the charges, perhaps with an eye on exposing the obvious failings of the proceedings in regard to the rights of the prisoners to a fair hearing (Michael Mallin). Miceál Ua hAnnracáin's short statement lay somewhere in the middle of this spectrum.

Found guilty of breaching Defence of the Realm Regulation 50, Miceál was sentenced to death, a sentence promptly confirmed by General Maxwell. In a certain sense, the British had got the right man. Outside of the Military Council of the IRB, there would have been few Volunteers more heavily involved in preparing for the insurrection than Miceál. No doubt, behind the scenes, the information provided by the 'G' men about Miceál's activities before the Rising helped inform Maxwell's memorandum to his Prime Minister that Miceál was 'one of the most active members' of the Volunteers and a 'constant associate' of the leaders of the Rising.[10] But in terms of the actual charge, the trial of Miceál Ua hAnnracáin was one of the clearest examples that demonstrate the proceedings were not genuine attempts to establish the truth but rather hurried formalities to clear the way for the executions that Maxwell wanted to carry out. No proof could be offered for Armstrong's assertion that Miceál was involved in causing casualties among British troops, because Miceál did not, in fact, participate in any fighting. It is no wonder that in 1917 the British government was advised not to make public the details of the trials as 'there are one or two cases in which the evidence is very thin'. The records of the proceedings were not released until 1999.[11]

That Wednesday evening, Miceál was transferred from Richmond Barracks to Kilmainham Jail, Cell Number 67, in preparation for his execution the following morning. Late in the day, the authorities contacted Miceál's family. Eily

O'Hanrahan recalled that terrible night in her statement for the Military Bureau in 1949.

On Wednesday night some time after we went to bed, probably between twelve and one, a lorry with military drove
up to the door accompanied by a car with a policeman
in it. They banged on the door, and at once the people
living opposite, Green was their name, put their heads out
the window. The military told them that if they did not
shut their windows and put out their lights they would do
it for them. We opened the door and the policeman gave
in a letter from the o.c. of Kilmainham, to the effect that
Micheál would like to see his mother and sisters before
his deportation to England. We decided we would not
let Mother come, as we thought it meant our arrest. The
policeman said we would be sorry if we did not take her.
We left Máire with Mother, and Cis [Anna] and I went,
under the impression that we were under arrest …

We were shown into a little white-washed room off the
hall, with two candles. We were sitting there for a while …

After a short time some soldiers came and brought us up
the dark iron stairs and along the iron corridor to Micheál's
cell. There was nothing in it, no light even, but an old bag
thrown in the corner, and a bucket, no bed, no chair, no
table, a place in which you would not put a dog. Micheál
was standing in the cell. When we rushed forward he caught

us in his arms. He asked us did we know the circumstances that brought us, and where was Mother. We told him why we had not brought her and we said we knew now why we had been sent for. He said he would have loved to see Mother and Máire, but that it was better after all Mother had not come. He was not in any way agitated. The only thing that worried him was what was to become of my mother and us. He said he did not know where Harry was. They were devoted to each other and did everything together. He told us not to fret, and we tried to reassure him that we would be all right and that the women of '98 had to endure that too. There were six soldiers and two officers, and any time we said anything referring to the Volunteers and the Movement, one of the officers came forward and said we must speak of nothing but personal matters. I mentioned that Tom Clarke and Pearse were gone and one of the officers interrupted me. Again in the course of conversation I mentioned that MacDonagh was gone and again I was stopped. We told him that Ned Daly and two others were going with himself. We rushed in all this information in a hurry and with the greatest difficulty. We were left there only a short time, although we had been told that the interview would be for 20 minutes. We asked to be permitted to stay to the end, but the officers said that would be out of the question. I asked Micheál if he had anything to eat. He said some bully-beef had been left to him in a billycan, but he had not eaten it. I asked had he not had a bed. He said no. Then one of the officers said to Micheál if he had any affairs to settle he should do so without delay. I said, how can anyone situated as he is without a table or chair even settle anything. A table and chair and a candle in an old candlestick were brought. It was then we saw how bad the cell really was. Micheál wrote his will on paper headed with the Kilmainham stamp. He left all he had – which was only his books – to Mother and to his sisters after her death. Only for that will we would not have afterwards got his medals, as a brother of ours who had married early and had no sympathy with Ireland applied for them, and the affair went on for months. The record of this is in the Department of Defence.

When he had finished the will he said he would be seeing father in a few hours. We asked him had he seen a priest. An officer said his clergy had been sent for and would be here presently. Micheál said he had asked for Fr Augustine and Fr Albert. These priests were marvelous. They saved the reason of many people whose sons and brothers were executed. Fr Aloysius and Fr Sebastian were very good too. The two former used to come and see us regularly, sometimes they came twice a day in a cab. The two officers witnessed the will. Although these men did their duty they were not aggressive.

We said goodbye to Micheál. He did not weep, but kept

up his courage. We did not give way either then. He kissed us several times and told us to give his love to Mother and Máire and to Harry when we found out where he was. I think he was afraid Harry would be executed too. We came downstairs and I got weak, and when I got to the ground floor I fainted. A stretcher was brought and I was laid on it. One of the soldiers, an Irishman, made himself very objectionable and seemed to gloat over the executions. When I became conscious again I was brought back to the same room we had been in before. One soldier – an Englishman – was very kind, he brought water and tried to console us. He said, 'after all ladies, your brother is getting the death he would have wished for'. As we were passing into the room Cis asked me, 'who is that girl sitting in the hall?' I said, 'that is Grace Gifford,' and while we were in the room we heard an officer ask her who she was. She answered, 'I am Mrs Plunkett'. We did not know she had been married.[12]

In addition to this account, Eily also shared her experience with Francis P Jones. In Jones's history of Sinn Féin, Miceál is reported as saying to his sisters in that meeting in his cell: 'I am ready to give my life for God and my country. In a few hours I shall be with my God, where I will plead the cause of my beloved Ireland and will ask God to bless mother and you.' The last words he spoke to his sisters were: 'Remember, girls, this is God's will, and it is for Ireland.'[13]

Alone once again, Miceál had only a few hours to think back over his life's path from a journeyman corkcutter in his childhood, to a full-time political activist in his mature years, to his development as a novelist. And to ponder too on the potential political consequences of the Rising. Would it inspire a new generation to the belief that British rule of Ireland could be broken? Would it encourage people to take matters into their own hands rather than wait in the hope that Britain might grant Home Rule?

While he lived out his final hours in Richmond Barracks and Kilmainham Jail, Miceál's former Redmondite associates from Carlow – people he had worked with on the '98 commemorations and in the Gaelic League – were urging the British authorities to deal severely with the ringleaders of the Rising. This was no local aberration. A few days earlier, on Saturday 29 April, John Redmond himself had offered the services of the Volunteers loyal to him to help fight against the rebels.[14] That this loyalty to the imperial authorities was soon to lead the Redmondites to disaster was quickly realised, and the Carlow District Council conveniently omitted to record in the minutes their vindictive resolution in an attempt to hide their condemnation of a figure who was soon to be celebrated as a local hero (too late, for the newspapers had recorded the meeting for perpetuity).[15] To judge by Miceál's comment to Harry – that the Rising had saved Ireland – he had already some premonition of the future trend of events. Certainly, he met his death with composure.

Just before dawn on Thursday 4 May 1916, Fr Augustine gave the last rites of the Church to Miceál:

> I saw O'Hanrahan for a short while in his cell … He was one of the truest and noblest characters that it has ever been my privilege to meet. His last message to me before he went out into the dark corridor that led to the yard where he was shot was: 'Father, I'd like you saw my mother and sisters and consoled them.' I promised him I would, and whispering something in his ear, I grasped the hands that were tied behind his back. In his right he pressed mine most warmly; we exchanged a look, and he went forth to die.[16]

That account was given by Fr Augustine to the Military Bureau in 1949. His more immediate account of the executions given to Aine Ceannt hinted at how disturbing he found the experience:

> He [Fr Augustine] accompanied Micheál from the cell to the yard, witnessed the execution and anointed him as he dropped. He did the same for each of the doomed men whom he attended … In every case it would appear as if it was necessary for the officer in charge of the firing party to dispatch the victim by a revolver shot. Father Augustine thought that this was a dreadful thing.[17]

Aine Ceannt's recollection of what Fr Augustine told her conforms to the unpleasant mockery of a red-haired Royal Irish Regiment sergeant who, as Liam Tannam – IRB member and Captain in Third Battalion – recounted, took great pleasure in coming around to the cells of the prisoners in Kilmainham and gloating that he had just been present at the firing squad and had seen brains splattered all over the wall.[18]

Chapter 10

• • • • •

The Aftermath

On the morning of Thursday 4 May, Eily and Anna met Fr Augustine in Church Street, and he tried to console them in their loss. 'They were very brave and grateful,' he recalled, 'especially when I promised that I would call as soon as possible to see their mother.'[1] First, though, Fr Augustine wanted to see Harry, who was also in Kilmainham under sentence of death. On learning of Miceál's death, Harry leaned his head against his right arm, which was pressed against the wall, and burst into tears and sobs for a while before recovering.[2] The two brothers were more than usually close: Eily described them as inseparable, saying that 'where Micheal led, Harry followed'.[3] The execution of Miceál was a mortal wound to Harry too, in the sense that from this moment his health went into decline and (weakened further by participation in two hunger strikes) he died prematurely in 1927.

Spared as a result of the growing outcry against the executions, Harry underwent the first of his several experiences of British prisons after his death sentence was commuted to incarceration for life and he was taken to Portland Prison, Dorset. From there he wrote home on 15 May 1916:

> The Sunday evening in which we surrendered, we marched to Richmond Barracks and the [officers?] and ourselves were trying to keep in a bunch, this we did until the detectives came about 2.00 and picked out about 14 including the 2 Cosgraves, T Mac Donagh, Kent ourselves and you know the results since we were picked out on Monday.
>
> We had 7 or 8 girls at Jacobs including Máire Walker, they were bricks. They were very good to poor Miceál and myself.
>
> Now in other … ask you not to fret about me. I am and will be alright please God and as for poor Miceál is he not better off? When we started we were all prepared to go under and had confession in Jacob's on the Tuesday and the Wednesday evenings that we were there. We had the priests very often. We had only one casualty there.[4]

Back at home, even though the family had paid the month's rent (£1, 11s.) on 67 Connaught Street, the landlady gave them notice to quit, fearing that the house would be blown up. The girls wanted to contest the notice but Mary, whose health was shaken, wished to stay out of trouble. Richard's brother from Wexford, the printer Watty Hanrahan, generously offered to buy the house if the family wanted to stay on. But with a collapse in the household income, Miceál's mother and sisters decided it would be better to move out and start a shop where they could hope to earn enough to keep themselves. So in November 1916, they took 384 North Circular Road, where they had a tobacco and general goods store downstairs and living rooms upstairs.[5]

At this address they produced (with the help of Watty's printing press) Miceál's speech to Cumann na mBan as a pamphlet and sold *A Swordsman of the Brigade*, but this effort to promote Miceál's works did not last long as the police and military raided the house often and took everything, including the stock of the shop. Miceál's surviving family came close to complete ruin.[6] After enduring a period of three weeks' solitary confinement, Harry obtained release from Portland as part of the general amnesty of prisoners rounded up in the rebellion, and on his return to Dublin on 18 June 1917, the family turned the corner and began to pick up business, especially with the support of Sinn Féin members.

Naturally, the O'Hanrahans were determined to continue the fight against British rule. Eily and Harry, in particular, worked almost full time for advanced nationalism; Harry was a leading figure in Sinn Féin, Inns Quay Cumann in Dublin, and, indeed, in the party nationally. In January 1922, Harry was elected to the fifteen-person standing committee of Sinn Féin, but unfortunately this was just as the party prepared to split over the Treaty.[7] Similarly, his role as a judge in the Dáil Courts, North City District (where he heard cases concerning non-payment of rent and possession), was cut short by the outbreak of the Civil War.[8]

From 1917, the O'Hanrahan house and shop began to fill up again in secret with arms and papers, with the dump being built into the roof. Being close to Mountjoy Prison, the shop was a useful place for organising messages and parcels to prisoners and to the GHQ of the reorganised IRA, who used the premises as a call office, dumping station, and depot. Some time during the hunger strike of Thomas Ashe (begun 28 May 1917), at Arthur Griffith's request, the dining room of the house was given up for the headquarters of Sinn Féin.[9] Also in 1917, during the South Longford election campaign in support of Joseph McGuinness (Sinn Féin) against Patrick McKenna (Irish Party) – the famous 'Vote Him In to Get Him Out' election – George Geraghty was seriously wounded during an attack on Sinn Féin HQ. He was attended to by Eily, who rendered first aid. Mary O'Hanrahan was also present, having come down with Eily to assist the campaign.[10]

The arms hidden at the house were constantly needed, mostly by the Second Battalion, Dublin, and Eily was kept busy bringing them to ambushes or funerals. As Eily recalled, 'If there was to be an ambush at, say, the Cross Guns Bridge, perhaps the men would come in and say, "would you deliver this to such a man?" I would have to do that immediately;

and the firing squads for the funerals, we used to have to be there in the Graveyard [Glasnevin].'[11]

Eily also played a large role in fundraising for men returned from prison. She would obtain spare suits from better-off members in order to provide clothing, and she organised collections at concerts and via sheets on the counter at the shop. Most importantly of all in their efforts to defeat the authorities responsible for the execution of their brother, Harry and Eily went on to play a crucial role in Michael Collins' battle against British intelligence thanks to the decision by Eamon Broy to use their shop as the key point for the transfer of his documents to Collins. Broy explained his choice to the Military Bureau:

I thought hard on this problem for a long time, and came to the decision that whoever I would deal with would have to be somebody extreme, who hated England and who would be prepared to take a chance. I finally decided that the best place to make such contact was through some nationalist's shop where callers would not attract any special notice. Weighing the merits of various shops controlled by nationalist sympathisers, I came finally to the conclusion that only two were possible, namely, JJ Walsh's of Blessington St and O'Hanrahan's of 384, North Circular Road … Michael O'Hanrahan had been executed in 1916. His brother, Harry O'Hanrahan, and two sisters ran the shop.

They were all, of course, what the police called 'notorious' Sinn Féiners. I myself could not dare to visit this shop.

... I thought of a Sinn Féiner who was married to a first cousin of mine. His name was Patrick Tracy and he was employed as a clerk at Kingsbridge railway terminus. I had a talk with Tracy, and he agreed to transfer any information I wanted transferred. He also agreed that O'Hanrahan's shop was ideal for the purpose.

... From that [time] on, every secret and confidential document, police code, etc. that came to my hands was sent, through Tracy and O'Hanrahan, to the Volunteer head-quarters. I knew nothing at all about Michael Collins. I understand that Greg Murphy did most of the transferring from O'Hanrahan's of the documents I gave, and that some documents went to Eamon Duggan and Harry Boland, but where they went, in the main, I never ascertained.[12]

Broy added, 'all the police reports ... were sent by me through O'Hanrahan's, usually on the very days the reports were typed'.[13] And, 'I furnished Volunteer Headquarters with all secret and confidential G. Division reports from 1917 to 1921. From 1917 to 1919 these reports passed mainly through the O'Hanrahan shop, and where they were taken eventually I never ascertained.' When he was not in an Eng-lish prison, Harry played a role in supplying this intelligence to Michael Collins, reading and discussing the material that arrived at the shop from Eamon Broy.[14] Eventually Broy met Collins personally and this direct relationship came about thanks to Harry O'Hanrahan.[15]

When Patrick Tracy first called to the shop to set up this line of communication, however, Eily was suspicious of him: 'I remember that a man called Tracy brought information from Broy. When he came first we did not like the look of him and we did not think he was to be trusted. We never, however, had any justifications for our suspicions and we never heard that he did anything against us or the Volunteers. But he did not impress us very favourably. I do not remember that we copied any messages he brought. Some of them were verbal.[16]

A buzzer system was installed in the shop by some IRA men to help avoid any of these crucial documents being discovered in the event of one of the many raids that took place. It was placed on the edge of the shop counter so that if someone serving leaned on it, the signal would sound deeper in the house and that would give a moment for anyone present to clear out. The signal for a raid was three rings of the buzzer.[17]

As a result of the secrecy needed in handling these documents, Eily had to withdraw from overt Cumann na mBan activity. This was later to lead to difficulties in her efforts to claim a military pension, despite the testimony of those still alive in the 1940s and 1950s who knew about her role in the intelligence system.

On 1 February 1920, in a 4am raid on the O'Hanrahan house, Harry was rearrested by a large military force. The soldiers refused to answer questions about where they were taking him, but it soon became known that these military raids had rounded up ten activists. Large crowds assembled at the docks the next morning in case the men were taken from the country, but there was no sign of them.[18] Harry was in fact in Mountjoy with the other men, who were never charged with any offence. Later, after the watch on the ferries had died away, they were smuggled out of the country by the authorities and incarcerated in solitary confinement in Wormwood Scrubbs, from where eventually Harry was allowed to write to his relatives and they to him, at least until the governor decided to restrict the correspondence on the grounds that it was straying beyond a 'personal, domestic or business nature'.

'The trouble is,' Eily told the *Sunday Independent*, 'that this is the first we heard about any rule. At any rate as you can see from the letters, which you are at perfect liberty to read, there is not a single thing in any of them that a sister ought not write to her brother. They are all about personal, domestic and business matters.'

'As things are at present,' she continued, 'we don't even know if our brother is at Wormwood Scrubbs, or where he is.'[19]

From 5 April 1920, a hunger strike by socialists and republicans being held without charge in Mountjoy led to a massive general strike across the country, with 'soviets' springing up to run the towns of Ireland while the strike took place. Stunned by these events and fearful of prolonging them, the British authorities caved in and released the men on 14 April 1920.[20] This result inspired the men in Wormwood Scrubbs to discuss whether to begin a hunger strike of their own, as Eamon O'Duibhir, County Centre, IRB Tipperary, recalled:

> Disunion arose in the Prison amongst our own fellows … on the question of having a hunger strike for release. One group said it would be wrong to stage a hunger strike for that purpose. We could not have it for anything else because we were being treated as prisoners of war, and Jim Lawless, Henry O'Hanrahan, P.J. Moloney and others insisted that it would be very wrong to have this hunger strike for release. On the other side we had the argument that the British had no right to keep us there. Why not get out of the place? Joe MacDonagh became the leader of what we will call the hunger strike men, and with him were Frank McGrath, myself, Eamon Hayes and, as a matter of fact, the majority of the prisoners …
>
> After a five day hunger strike we were not too strong but we managed to wreck the prison before we had to sit down or lie down completely exhausted. We were pleased to find that all our old comrades, those who had not been on hunger strike, had now joined in the struggle, so we

were a united party once more.

On the 27th and 28th April a large crowd of sympathisers gathered in Wormwood Scrubbs Common outside the prison. On the first night they were attacked by a mob from the city. On the second night a large crowd of Irishmen came there with hurleys, ashplants or blackthorns or canes of some kind and we understood that a good deal of English workers aided them to rout this mob.[21]

The hunger strike achieved its aim, in that the men were released in small groups, but only after they had almost reached the point of death. Harry, who had many followers, had been 'dead against' the hunger strike and argued that no central authority had given the go-ahead to it. Nevertheless, once the hunger strike was underway, Harry led his men in joining it with great determination, even if it shattered his health.[22] Nor was there much of a period of recuperation at home by Harry on his return to Ireland, for almost immediately he went on the run to avoid being targeted by the military. At that time too, more and more raids were mounted on 384 North Circular Road, culminating in a vicious ransacking of the house in August 1920.

This was not, however, the worst experience of the period for the family. That came in 1922, with the cruel irony that so many encountered during the Civil War, when the former comrades of Harry and the O'Hanrahan sisters bombed the premises. This attack on their home was due to the fact that the family had taken an anti-Treaty stance.

On Sunday 2 April 1922, with Commandant Peadar Kearney presiding, Harry gave a speech after Mass in Dunmanway in County Cork in support of the Republican policy, and on the same day he gave an address from a wagon in the Market Place, Bandon. In his speech, he said, 'Who were the people in Co. Cork who were backing up the Treaty? You will find that it is the landlords and the shoneens who were always against you. They have now got rid of the landlords to a great extent, but if that Treaty is passed it means bringing back landlords and bodies will be manned by Unionists and such. Look at the men who were appointed to draw up the Constitution – deputy-lieutenants ... The way to prevent civil war was to return Republican candidates at the election.'[23]

The family, and especially Eily, were heavily involved in supporting the Republicans when the war began. Eily was on duty at Tara Hall, Gloucester Street, and afterwards, from 28 June 1922, at a first-aid dressing station in North Great Georges Street during the opening week of the Battle for Dublin in the Civil War. There she attended the wounded and did general nursing. Harry fought in the Hammam Hotel in O'Connell Street. Thereafter, Eily and Harry supported the Republicans, with their house once again used for the custody of arms, documents, records and the holding of meetings. In 1922, the *Republican War News* was printed in the drawing room of the house and delivered all over the country. At one point, Eily was taken to Mountjoy but was released soon after, having gone on hunger strike.[24]

Edward, the brother who had remained behind in Carlow when the rest of the family moved to Dublin and who was not politically active, also inadvertently got caught up in Civil War politics in 1922, on the other side to that of his brother and sisters. When, in September 1922, the new Irish Free State government set out to smash the postal workers union, Edward and one other person in the large staff at Galway, where he was assigned at the time, announced that they intended to cross picket lines the following day in order to provide a few hours of essential service.[25] That night (14 September 1922) a heavy stone was thrown through the window of Edward's cottage and crashed on the floor of the bedroom where the children were sleeping. Earlier that day a deputation of strikers had visited O'Hanrahan, and whoever had thrown the stone had done so without approval from the unions, who condemned the attack. Two days later, the Free State promoted Edward to the postmastership of Greystones, County Wicklow.[26]

In the elections of 30 August 1923, Harry stood as an anti-Treaty candidate in Dublin North. He obtained 646 votes on the first count, well short of the quota of 6,147. Thereafter he drew back from politics due to ill health – in

1926 he underwent two serious operations in the Mater to attempt to address his bouts of severe stomach pain – and the O'Hanrahans concentrated on trying to build up a business. For a while they did well, specialising in gramophones and radios: they were the sole agent in Leinster for Marconi radios and were able to open up a shop on O'Connell Street.[27] This knowledge of modern broadcasting equipment was put behind the then-radical Fianna Fáil party when, during the election campaign in June 1937, a huge rally was held in Dublin. The provision of loudspeakers by the O'Hanrahan sisters allowed the gathering to hear the speeches distinctly.[28]

By this time, the sisters were alone and struggling to make ends meet. Mary had died in 1925; she was buried in Glasnevin Cemetery and the occasion drew a large attendance, with figures such as Éamon de Valera, Austin Stack, Fr O'Flanagan, Oscar Traynor, Dan Breen, Kathleen Clarke and Seamus Brennan among the mourners. Harry died of secondary carcinoma of the liver (the cancer presumably having spread from his bowel) in the Mater Hospital, Dublin, on 20 September 1927. He had never been the same since Miceál's execution. He too was buried at Glasnevin, and his funeral was attended by his old comrades of the IRA.

For all three sisters, a military pension was essential to keep them from poverty. The gramophone business, which had been so promising, lost headway as a result of a fire in the O'Hanrahans' O'Connell Street shop in 1935.

As Éamon de Valera wrote when asked to support their claims, 'For years some of [Harry's] sisters seem to have been in needy circumstances and I regret I cannot give any testimony which might be of assistance to them.'[29] Áine initially tried, but failed, to claim a pension as a dependent upon Harry in 1954, explaining that 'my circumstances are anything but good and were it not that I am living with my married sister and her husband, things would be indeed bad for me.'[30] Thanks to the 1962 Act, Áine eventually obtained a pension in her own right for her activities with Cumann na mBan. Máire had earlier done the same under the 1952 Act.

The secret nature of Eily's work in the 1917–1921 period counted against her as it led to scepticism by the pension adjudicators, who also made a note of her Republican views. Eily struggled to win the award she felt entitled to. As she put it in a bitter letter to the Pensions Board: 'I am reluctantly compelled now to feel that the Board or its Advisors are either dubious of my service or are refraining from granting my pension, because they feel that other cases are more deserving owing to their immediate hardships, and I am sorry to say that if they only knew the circumstances and the hardships that the sisters of Miceal and Harry O'Hanrahan are now going through they would think differently … If the O'Hanrahan family could even get a living in this country I would not trouble you, but I am depending on the pension to keep a roof over our heads, until the good God takes us to meet the dead patriots of 1916.' Eily had to wait six years from her first pension claim in 1928, until the Act of 1934, to obtain an award of just over five years' service (then worth £25:5:6) following her appeal against the original award. Even this represented an under-appreciation of a role that is now more visible thanks to the evidence in the Military Bureau.[31]

While the fortunes of Miceál's sisters were precarious, Edward O'Hanrahan reached the post of Assistant Superintendent, Controller's Branch, GPO, College Green. He died on 15 October 1941 in Dublin. Miceál's three sisters all had long lives and lived into the 1970s. Áine O'Hanrahan died on 16 September 1973; Eily O'Hanrahan died on 24 September 1974; and Máire O'Hanrahan, the last of Miceál's siblings, died on 18 February 1975. They lived long enough to see that as the 'old crowd' became fewer and fewer over time, the social memory of the role that Miceál had played in the Easter Rising diminished. In part, this was a consequence of his unassuming character and in part a consequence of the secretive roles that he undertook. The relative lack of public recognition for his part in the Rising should not be considered a reflection on Miceál's actual importance to the events of 1916.

Miceál Ua hAnnracáin was an extremely modest man whose greatest ambition from a very early age was to free Ireland from the Imperial administration. Underneath a reserved exterior was a passion and a drive that meant Miceál gave up nearly every evening of his adult life to one organisation or another that furthered this goal. From his journalism it is clear that Miceál read carefully into Ireland's history – and the history of other countries within the Empire – and came to the conclusion that the attempt of the Imperial administration to portray itself as a benevolent influence upon Irish affairs was a lie. His belief was that when their interests were threatened, the supporters of the Empire were savage in their barbarity. In Carlow, for example, a terrible massacre had been carried out in 1798 against the United Irishmen and Miceál helped preserve the memory of this event.

Whether from his own natural disposition, or from the experience of his father in the old IRB of '67, Miceál operated as covertly as he could against a very powerful enemy, one that he believed would never voluntarily surrender control of Ireland to the Irish people. As with many of his contemporaries, Miceál was convinced that the British Empire had to be defeated militarily if Ireland were to escape its domination. Due to this belief, to his discretion, and to his scrupulous honesty and willingness to devote all his time to the revolutionary movement, Miceál became the key figure behind the scenes in arming and equipping the Volunteers. He had developed the skills to do this task effectively in the course of organising for the Gaelic League, Sinn Féin and especially the great language processions.

As Easter 1916 approached, Miceál had high hopes for the ability of the Irish Volunteers to inflict a stunning blow on the Imperial administration, hopes that were shattered by the loss of the *Aud*. When given the news that the 20,000 rifles had not been landed, Miceál was as shaken as he had ever been in his life and must have had a premonition of his own death, for the odds of victory suddenly lengthened enormously. They lengthened again when MacNeill issued his countermanding order. The members of the Military Council of the IRB were then in a terrible position: they were faced with very little chance of victory, but with the certainty of humiliation and massive damage to the credibility of the IRB and those who had built the Irish Volunteers if they did not fight.

Desmond Ryan remembered the conversations among the revolutionaries at this time and their concern that if the Rising did not go ahead, 'the spring of the whole Irish-Ireland movement might snap, and nothing would ever in our lifetimes mend it again. Yet it seemed as if the whole chance of striking first had gone, and we talked and talked round it.'[32] In the event, Miceál, like so many of the other leaders of the rebellion, went out with little hope of victory, but with a determination to create the circumstances, even in defeat, that would 'save Ireland'. As he awaited his execution, he believed that those who fought in the Easter Rising had achieved this much at least. Calm and unwavering in the face of death, it seems that he was satisfied that it was worth his life to have helped bring about a fundamental change in political direction for the country, one that would lead to more successful struggles in the future.

In different circumstances, Miceál Ua hAnnracáin would have indulged his love of literature and lived a long life devoted to writing novels. This, however, was not an ambition he could allow himself to yield to while the British Empire remained in control of Ireland. Instead, in a quiet and indefatigable manner, he put his considerable organisational talents and, ultimately, his life, at the disposal of the cause of national revolution.

Appendix

• • • • •

'Patches'

by Miceál Ua hAnnracáin

'Whoop! Whoop! Whoop!' rang out a stentorian voice, and through the entry came rushing a clown, his face white and ghastly, on his cheek-bones two round patches of black paint, his dress a wonderful thing of stripes and patches. With a final somersault he landed in the centre of the ring, and stood bowing.

'Patches! Patches!' came a greeting yell from all sides, as the juvenile audience rose to its feet, cheering wildly. It was school day at the Grand Continental Circus, and the young-sters, rejoicing in their half-day's freedom from irksome tasks and dull routine, were enjoying themselves in the uncritical spirit of the young.

Producing from his capacious pockets a collection of small instruments, the clown imitated the cries of various animals. His audience slowly resumed their seats, and sat mute and irresponsive. Their hero was not coming up to their expectations. But suddenly out from the entry a black-clad figure came bounding, and struck the clown, who had paused for an instant, a resounding blow on the cheek. A shout of surprise and anger rose from the audience.

'Coward! Coward!' the cries rang out.

Patches, reeling backward, disappeared for an instant within the entry, only to re-appear again brandishing a stick, from the end of which dangled a painted bladder. With a yell of affright the other fled before him. Round and round the ring they went, Patches belabouring his assailant about the head and shoulders, and all the while whooping terribly.

The delighted audience shouted encouragingly to their hero. The vast building rang. Here was a performance which appealed to all. Especially was one brown-haired little fellow noticeable by the abandon of his delight. His eyes sparkled and danced as he shouted:

'Give it to him, Patches. Give it to him: he struck first.'

Suddenly the pursued tripped and fell prostrate. With a triumphant cry Patches planted his foot on the prostrate form, and folding his arms looked around. He acknowledged the plaudit of his admirers by a bow; then permitting his fallen foe to rise to his feet, pointed dramatically to the entry, exclaiming: 'Begone, villain!'

Staggering, with his head hanging dejectedly, the defeated one disappeared amidst a storm of groans and hisses from the youngsters, who either praise or blame wholeheartedly. Stepping to the centre of the ring the victor stood bowing, while from the audience came saluting yells of 'Patches! Patches! Hurrah for Patches!'

Their hero was supreme. With a final flourish of his weapon he disappeared through the entry, but again and again had to make another bow to his young admirers. At last to the strains of 'Home, sweet Home,' the audience, chattering and talking, filed out, and homewards. The circus was over.

Let us follow the brown-haired youngster who had made himself so conspicuous by his cheering. He was only a little lad about nine or ten years of age, the son of a poor labourer, Art Maloney, who had found it difficult enough to spare out of his meager wages the two pence which brought his little boy to the circus. Walking as if on air, the youngster made his way through the crowded streets, going over the performance he had just witnessed. To him it was an experience which came all too seldom, for with the poor every penny counts. There is little fear of their children becoming sated through a plethora of amusements. Before the mind's eye of the child one figure stood out prominently, the grotesque figure of Patches. Him he deified, thought of to the exclusion of everything else; and when at last he turned in at the door of the little cottage out by the East Wall, where a tired, pale woman awaited him, he remembered only Patches. To her, eagerly questioning, he could speak only of Patches, and when his father came in later one he was still full of his hero.

'Daddy,' he exclaimed, while his eyes sparkled, 'when can I go again?'

'Heaven knows,' muttered the father. Aloud he said: 'As soon as I have one good week we'll all go.'

The youngster uttered an exclamation of delight.

'I hope it will be soon,' he said. 'I want to see Patches again.'

But the father made no reply. That night when the little boy had been tucked away in bed he dreamt of Patches. He seemed to stand before him, flourishing his painted bladder. Again the shouts of his companions saluting their hero rang in his ears. With a loud cry of 'Patches! Patches!' he started up. But the vision had faded. Only the darkness of the night was there. He heard only the regular breathing of his parents who, tired out after the toils of the day, slept on. Then, a little frightened at the blackness, he pulled the clothes over his head, and again slept.

II

Sadness was in the house by the East Wall. The brown-haired youngster, the admirer of Patches, lay in the grip of some strange malady. He had returned from school a few days previously, drenched through. The result of his wetting was sickness, during which he hovered between life and death. For three days and nights the anxious father and mother had watched by the bedside of the little invalid, giving him the medicines which the old doctor they had called in had recommended. Through his sickness the little boy had raved and talked. The name of Patches was constantly on his lips. Towards morning of the third night the fever abated, and then the little form lay inert, motionless, scarcely seeming to breathe. It almost seemed as if the child were dead. But no. When the doctor called, he expressed himself as very well satisfied with the improvement in his little patient. The fever had left him, but he was very weak.

'A few days more,' he said, 'and he will be running round again.'

Some time later when the father, tired and weary after his night's vigil, had gone away to his work, the child sat up suddenly. With a cry of affright the mother rushed to the bedside:

'What ails my pet?' she asked anxiously.

'Mammy,' said the little fellow, and she had to stoop to catch his words: 'I want to see Patches. The other day I watched all day at the Rotunda to see him. But it came on to rain, and I had to run home.'

'And who is Patches?' asked the mother.

'Sure, don't you know the clown I was telling you about the other day, that I saw at the circus,' replied the child, looking at her with wondering eyes, as if reproaching her for her want of knowledge of his hero.

'Oh, now I remember,' replied the mother. 'And you wanted to see him?'

'Yes,' replied the little fellow. 'I offered them a ha'penny to let me in, but they wouldn't.'

'Well, maybe you'll see him before long,' said the poor mother, kissing him. 'But you must get well before you can see him again.'

'Yes,' he answered, 'I must see him again.'

Since then, now a week ago, he had lain in a listless state, taking no interest in anything. Several times he asked if he could see Patches, but the poor parents had only evasive replies to give him. How were they to satisfy his strange longing? The old doctor could do nothing against this strange malady. And thus the little fellow sank and grew weaker from day to day. One night the medico took the big, burly father who was regarding his little son with sombre eyes, aside, and said:

'If your child is not roused from this state into which he has fallen he will die. I can do nothing. This man of whom he speaks – if you can find him, and satisfy the child's craving he will be saved. If not –,' and he went away shaking his head portentously.

Aye, if he could satisfy his craving. But how? As he looked at the wan little face on the pillow he saw how useless it would be to attempt to bring him to the circus. But a thought struck him. What not substitute this Patches? Had he not often see toy clowns in the shop windows? He would buy one of these. He had no doubt it would satisfy his son's yearning. Eagerly he told his wife of the idea. She approved, and, pressing a couple of sixpences into his hand, hurried him of. When he returned his face was flushed with excitement and hope. He carried a long brown paper parcel. The big man's hands shook as he unrolled the wrappings. There lay a 'Patches' in embryo, with painted cheeks and dress of many hues. Surely this effigy of his hero would cause his little boy to jump with delight. With bated breath he watched as the mother held the puppet before the little invalid, crying: 'See what your father has bought you. The "Patches" you were asking for.'

The little boy sat up. For an instant he seemed to rouse himself. Then with a hopeless cry of: 'That's not Patches. I'll never see him again,' he sank back on his pillows, and burst into bitter tears.

The poor mother covered her face with her apron, and sobbed out her anguish and disappointment. The father bit his lip savagely, and turned away quickly to hide his agitation. Naught could save their child now, it seemed. Their plan had failed. They could only wait and watch him die. But the voice of the sobbing woman came to him: 'Oh,' she cried in her anguish, 'if he could only see this Patches.'

With a flash of determination he turned towards her: 'I'll bring him here,' he cried.

She gazed at him, hardly understanding, and he hurried

on: 'I'll go to the Rotunda, and see this clown.'

'But he may not come,' said the poor woman despond-ently.

'He may have a child of his own,' he replied. 'I'll tell him all. We must do all we can to save him.'

'Well, go then in God's name,' she consented.

Poor Art almost ran to the Rotunda, such was his eager-ness. It was drawing near eleven o'clock, and he feared that the clown might have gone away. As he hurried along, the difficulty of the task he had set himself presented itself more clearly. He did not even know the name of the man he sought. How was he to find him amongst the large circus company? At the thought he stopped, and began to retrace his footsteps. But the wan face of his little son rose before him, and his insistent cry of 'Patches! Patches!' rang in his ears.

'I'll find him,' he muttered, turning his face northwards.

For several minutes he stood outside the Rotunda, under-neath the great flaring lights trying to think of some plan by which he might achieve his object. He gazed up at the gaudy pictures, and read through the announcements, but they afforded little real clue to the man he sought. And time was hurrying on. Already some of the audience were hurry-ing out giving warning that the performance was nearing its close. In desperation Art went in. He was stopped by a tall, broad-shouldered attendant.

'What do you want?' he asked, looking at Art suspiciously.

'I want to see a clown called "Patches",' replied Art.

'No one of the name here,' replied the other loftily, and turned away.

'Could you not try?' urged Art, seeing his last chance slipping from him. 'There is some clown of the name here, and I must see him.'

'Didn't you hear what I said?' snapped the be-laced man. 'Get out of this. I'm not here to answer drunken men. Here, get out,' and he seized Art by the shoulder.

But Art was fighting for the little life ebbing away at home. He struggled vigorously. The attendant was a powerful man, and so Art was being forced outside when a loud voice cried:

'Stop! What's all this about?'

Letting go his hold the be-laced one told his story, and then the newcomer, a stout man with a wonderful expanse of shirt-front, a double chin, and good-humoured face turned to Art, inquiring, 'Now, my man, what have you to say for yourself?'

Art hurried through his story. He told of his son lying sick, perhaps dying, at home; of the doctor's words, of his little boy's desire to see Patches.

'Maybe it might save him,' the poor father wound up.

'It might,' replied the stout man thoughtfully. 'But "Patches"! Well, we'll see.'

And he led Art through a glass door into an inner room, then hurried away telling him he would see if there might

227

be such a person in the company. Only a few moments had elapsed when a firmly built man with grey hair and twinkling eyes presented himself before him. He was dressed in a suit of greyish tweed, and bowler hat, and to Art's unaccustomed eyes looked very unclown-like indeed.

'Our manager has sent me to you,' he said. 'And I've only a few minutes to spare, for it's just closing time.'

'Are you Patches?' asked Art.

'I have been called by that name,' replied the other.

'Then I want to ask you a favour,' said Art, taking his courage in both hands. 'It means the saving of my little son from certain death.'

'But I'm not a doctor,' exclaimed the clown. 'I'm only a clown.'

'You are the doctor I want,' returned Art. 'Ten days ago my little son saw you performing here in the circus. A few days afterwards he offered a ha'penny, all the money he had, to get in to see you. That day he got drenched through and through, and now lies at home weak and ill. He calls out night and day for you. We have given him toys, but it is no use. We can't rouse him. The doctor says if we could let him have what he craves for he would recover.'

'And he wants to see me?' queried the clown.

'Yes, sir, he calls your name night and day. But we can't bring him here he is so weak –' and poor Art stopped short twisting his hat nervously in his hands.

'And you wish that I should go to him. Is that it?' asked the clown.

'Ah, sir, if you only would. He's only a little fellow, our only child. And maybe you have a little boy yourself.'

For an instant the clown turned away. When he turned again his rubicund face was pale, and he spoke in a soft, subdued voice which trembled slightly.

'Aye, I had once.' His eyes had a far-away, dreamy look, and he seemed not be aware of the other's presence. Perhaps he gazed into the long gone past to a cot where a little child with golden curls lay gasping in the throes of diphtheria. But he roused himself.

'Come,' he said to Art. 'We'll see what Dr. Patches can do.' A swift walk brought them to the cottage by the East Wall. The father hurried eagerly to the bedside of the child.

'Here,' he cried. 'Here is your friend, Patches.'

The little invalid raised his eyes listlessly to the smiling face of the stranger. But no light of recognition leaped into them. Instead, he turned his face to the wall, and wailed out in a hopeless, mournful voice:

'I'll never see Patches again. I'll never see Patches again.'

For a few moments Patches regarded the child earnestly, then turning away, he whispered to the father who was looking on with sombre eyes:

'Have no fear. He will see Patches. I will return as speedily as possible.'

Before Art had time to utter the words of thanks which sprang to his lips he was gone. Almost an hour had elapsed when the clown again made his appearance. He was enveloped from head to heel in a long coat. As he entered the outer apartment he threw off the long coat, and with a loud whoop sprang into the room where the child lay.

At the sound the youngster sat up erect. Before him he beheld the true Patches – the Patches for whom he had craved – flourishing his painted bladder, his face ghastly, on his cheek-bones the black spots, dressed in the motley garb just as if he stood in the ring of the Grand Continental Circus. Spellbound the little fellow sat gazing; then with a sigh of content he took the hand of his mother who had stolen silently to the bedside, and said in her ear, bent to catch his low-toned words:

'Mammy, I'll get well now, and then we can go to the circus to see Patches.'

And the clown, laying his hand on the curly head, exclaimed:

'Aye, Dr. Patches will be very glad to see his little patient.'

Notes

Chapter 1

1 Joseph McCarthy, BMH.WS1497, p. 1.

2 Eily O'Hanrahan, quoted in Larry Larkin, 'Ross Recollections', *New Ross Standard*, 6 August 1948.

3 Tomas Ua Raghallaigh, letter to the *Irish Press*, 28 March 1966.

4 *Irish Independent*, 4 May 1966.

5 Death Certificates: Richard, born to Mary Williams and Richard Hanrahan, 1 March 1871, New Ross. Died 1871, aged 0. Richard, born to Mary Williams and Richard Hanrahan, 25 March 1872, New Ross, aged 0. Both were available at http://www.irish genealogy.ie/en/ but in July 2014 the Civil Records Search was temporarily suspended.

6 Birth cert: Henry; Michael; Edward; death cert Richard. All were available at http://www.irishgenealogy.ie/en/.

7 Marriage cert was available at http://www.irishgenealogy.ie/en/. Eily O'Hanrahan-O'Reilly in 'Ross Recollections', *New Ross Standard*, 6 August 1948.

8 Birth cert was available at http://www.irishgenealogy.ie/en/.

9 Seamus Pender, ed. *A Census of Ireland circa 1659* (Dublin, 1939). My thanks to Michael O'Hanrahan for this information.

10 John O'Hart, *Irish Pedigrees 2* (fifth edition: Dublin, 1892) 1.209–10.

11 Alice Tracey, unpublished manuscript version of *Carloviana: Journal of the Old Carlow Society*, Vol. I, No. 12, (1963); with thanks to Michael and Pat Purcell.

12 http://www.rootsweb.ancestry.com/~irlcar2/tullow_st3.htm, accessed 13 June 2014. *The Nationalist and Leinster Times*, 21 December 1895.

13 http://www.census.nationalarchives.ie/reels/nai000419050/, accessed 13 June 2014.

14 http://www.cso.ie/ accessed 25 June 2014.

15 http://civilrecords.irishgenealogy.ie/churchrecords/details-civil/a9d26c8897964 and http://civilrecords.irishgenealogy.ie/churchrecords/details-civil/a1fad019408232 accessed 8 July 2014.

16 http://www.census.nationalarchives.ie/pages/1901/Carlow/Carlow/Tullow_ Street/1041265/, accessed 13 June 2014.

17 Fr Michael O'Flanagan in Miceál Ua hAnnracáin, *Irish Heroines* (Dublin, 1917), p. 3.

18 *Birmingham Daily Post*, 1 April 1891. Cited at http://corkcutter.info/, accessed 13 June 2014.

19 http://boards.ancestry.com/surnames.avern/7.1.1/mb.ashx, accessed 13 June 2014.

20 http://www.cbscarlow.ie/SchoolHistory.aspx, accessed 13 June 2014.

21 *Irish Independent*, 4 May 1966.

Chapter 2

1 *Gaelic Journal*, Vol. 1, 1882.

2 *The Irish Volunteer*, Vol 1.1, 7 February 1914.

3 TG McMahon, *Grand Opportunity: The Gaelic Revival and Irish Society, 1893–1910* (Syracuse, NY, 2008), p. 10.

4 *Fáinne an Lae*, 19 March 1898.

5 Fr Michael O'Flanagan in Miceál Ua hAnnracáin, *Irish Heroines*, p. 3.

6 Brian Higgins, ed., *Wolfe Tone Annual*, 1960, p. 42.

7 Brian Ó Cuív, 'Irish Language and Literature, 1845–1921' in W E Vaughan (ed.), *Ireland Under the Union*, II, NHI 6 (Oxford, 1995), pp. 385–435, here pp. 410–11.

8 *Sunday Independent*, 30 June 1912; *Southern Star*, 6 July 1912.

9 *Fáinne an Lae*, 2 April 1898.

10 *The Nationalist and Leinster Times*, 16 April 1898.

11 Tom Little, note in Michael Purcell, 'Carlow – The Provincial Leader in a Gaelic Revival', *Carloviana* 31 (1983), pp. 6–7, here p. 7.

12 *Fáinne an Lae*, March 25 1899.

13 TG McMahon, *Grand Opportunity*, pp. 95–8.

14 Sean O'Casey, *Drums Under the Windows, Autobiography,* Book 3 (Dublin, 1945), p. 3.

15 Mary Butler, 'Women's Role in Sustaining Gaelic Culture', in Alan O'Day & John Stevenson, eds., *Irish Historical Documents Since 1800* (Dublin, 1992), p. 133.

16 TG McMahon, *Grand Opportunity*, p. 110. *An Claidheamh Soluis*, 25 September 1911.

17 *Fáinne an Lae*, 19 March 1898.

18 http://www.census.nationalarchives.ie/pages/1901/Carlow/Carlow/Dublin_Road/1040839/, accessed 16 June 2014.

19 http://www.census.nationalarchives.ie/pages/1901/Carlow/Carlow/Pollerton_ Little/1040294/, accessed 16 June 2014.

20 http://www.census.nationalarchives.ie/pages/1901/Carlow/Carlow/Charlotte_ Street/1040745/, accessed 16 June 2014.

21 http://www.census.nationalarchives.ie/pages/1901/Carlow/Leighlinbridge/ Ballyknocken/1043181/, accessed 16 June 2014.

22 http://www.census.nationalarchives.ie/pages/1901/Carlow/Carlow/Mill_ Lane/1041019/, accessed 16 June 2014.

23 http://www.census.nationalarchives.ie/pages/1901/Carlow/Carlow/Carlow_ Urban/1040688/, accessed 16 June 2014.

24 *An Claidheamh Soluis*, 25 June 1904; *Irish Freedom*, April 1911.

25 *Fáinne an Lae*, 19 March 1898.

26 *Fáinne an Lae*, 9 April 1898.

27 *The Nationalist and Leinster Times*, 30 April 1898.

28 *The Nationalist and Leinster Times*, 28 May 1898.

29 *The Nationalist and Leinster Times*, 4 June 1898.

30 *The Nationalist and Leinster Times*, 30 July 1898.

31 *The Nationalist and Leinster Times*, 8 May 1916.

Chapter 3

1 *An Claidheamh Soluis*, 18 March 1899.

2 *An Claidheamh Soluis*, 25 March 1899.

3 *An Claidheamh Soluis*, 8 April 1899.

4 Fr Michael O'Flanagan in Miceál Ua hAnnracáin, *Irish Heroines*, p. 3.

5 James McGuire & James Quinn, eds., *Dictionary of Irish Biography*, 7 (Cambridge, 2009), pp. 525–6; Alice Tracy, 'Michael O'Hanrahan', *Carloviana*, i (Dec. 1963), 12, 13, 38–9.

6 *An Claidheamh Soluis*, 17 June 1899.

7 *Proceedings of the Third Oireachtas*, 1899, p. 9; p. 23.

8 *Ibid*. p. 10.

9 TG McMahon, *Grand Opportunity*, pp. 88, 157.

10 Brian Ó Cuív, *Irish Language and Literature, 1845–1921*, p. 411.

11 *An Claidheamh Soluis*, 22 April 1899.

12 *An Claidheamh Soluis*, 13 May 1899.

13 *An Claidheamh Soluis*, 22 July 1899.

14 *An Claidheamh Soluis*, 30 June 1906.

15 *Fáinne an Lae*, 19 March 1899.

16 *Fáinne an Lae*, 26 May 1900.

17 *Fáinne an Lae*, 15 July 1900.

18 *Fáinne an Lae*, September 2 1899.

19 *An Claidheamh Soluis*, 12 May 1899.

20 *Fáinne an Lae*, 19 August 1899.

21 *Fáinne an Lae*, 26 August 1899.

22 *Fáinne an Lae*, 9 September 1899.

Chapter 4

1 Laurence Marlow, *The Working Men's Club Movement, 1862–1912: a study of a working class institution* (Unpublished PhD thesis, University of Warwick, 1980), p. 182.

2 MJ Kelly, *The Fenian Ideal and Irish Nationalism, 1882–1916* (Woodbridge, 2006), p. 53.

3 *Minute Book of Carlow Workingman's Club, 1899–1915*, Microfilm, NLI.

4 *Ibid*.

5 *Ibid*.

6 Michael Purcell, 'Michael O'Hanrahan and the Workman's Club', *Carlow Advertiser*, 9 June 1983.

7 *Minute Book of Carlow Workingman's Club, 1899–1915*.

8–16 *Ibid*.

17 MJ Kelly, *The Fenian Ideal and Irish Nationalism*, p. 153.

18 *Minute Book of Carlow Workingman's Club, 1899–1915*.

19 *Ibid*.

20 Eily O'Hanrahan O'Reilly, BMH.WS0270, p. 1.

21 *The Kerryman*, 9 April 1966.

22 Fr Michael O'Flanagan in Miceál Ua hAnnracáin, *Irish Heroines*, p. 3.

23 Kitty O'Doherty, BMH.WS0355, p. 8.

24 *New Ross Standard*, 6 August 1948.

25 Eily O'Hanrahan O'Reilly, BMH.WS0270, p. 10.

Chapter 5

1 Harry C. Phibbs, BMH.WS0848, pp. 10–11.

2 Seamus Ua Caomhanaigh, BMH.WS0889, p. 22.

3 *Ibid*. p. 11.

4 Máire O'Hanrahan's application for 'Dependent's Allowance or Gratuity', Memo 28
   January 1954 in Military Service Pensions Collection, 1D445, available at
   http://mspcsearch.militaryarchives.ie/docs/files//PDF_Pensions/1/1D445Michael
   OHanrahan/W1D445MichaelOHanrahan.pdf . Accessed 23 June 2015.

5 *Thom's* Directory, 1911. Harry C. Phibbs, BMH.WS0848, p. 11.

6 *The Harp*, June 1908.

7 MJ Kelly, *The Fenian Ideal and Irish Nationalism*, p. 140.

8 MJ Kelly, *The Fenian Ideal and Irish Nationalism*, pp. 141–2.

9 MJ Kelly, *The Fenian Ideal and Irish Nationalism*, p. 142.

10 Proinnsias O Dubhthaigh, BMH.WS0654, pp. 12–13.

11 Eily O'Hanrahan, quoted in Larry Larkin, 'Ross Recollections', *New Ross Standard*,
   6 August 1948.

12 Frank Henderson in Military Service Pensions Collection, DP25774, Henry
   O'Hanrahan, available at http://mspcsearch.militaryarchives.ie/detail.
   aspx?parentpriref=. Accessed 15 October 2014.

13 See, for example, the experience of TJ Meldon, BMH.WS0734, p. 12.

14 *Freeman's Journal,* 25 April 1908.

15 *The Times*, 22 July 1903.

16 http://www.adams.ie/DENIS-PHELAN-ARCHIVE-Phelan-Denis-
   1880-1976-Sinn-Fein-Donegal-An-important-collection-of-documents-
   membership-cards-letters-and-medals-relating-to-Denis-Phelan-a-life-long-
   Republican-from-Co-Tyrone-bo?Itemid=&view=lot_detail. Accessed 23 June 2015.

17 Tom Johnson archive, Letter to Liam de Roiste 20/10/1906.

18 *Freeman's Journal*, 12 January 1906.

19 *Freeman's Journal*, 13 January 1906.

20 Harry C. Phibbs, BMH.WS0848, p. 11.

21 *The Peasant – And Irish Ireland*, May 4 1907.

22 PS O'Hegarty, Arthur Griffith, *Studies: An Irish Quarterly Review*, pp. 852–855, here p. 854.

23 Cahir Healy, 'Notes on Reminiscences', Public Record Office of N. Ireland, Cahir Healy papers, D2991/C/1 in Eamon Phoenix, 'Cahir Healy (1877-1970): Northern Nationalist Leader', *Clogher Record*, 18. 1 (2003), 32–52, here p. 35.

24 For example, Seosamh Ua Ruairc, BMH.WS1244, p. 2.

25 Fr Michael O'Flanagan in Miceál Ua hAnnracáin, *Irish Heroines*, p. 3; *Skibbereen Eagle*, 24 August 1907.

26 Francis P Jones, *History of the Sinn Féin Movement and the Irish Rebellion of 1916* (New York: 1917), p. 167.

27 *Irish Press*, 5 May 1966.

28 *Irish Freedom*, November 1910.

29 For example, his articles in *Irish Freedom*, January 1911, May 1911.

30 *Irish Freedom*, May 1911.

31 *Donegal News*, 28 May 1904.

32 *Freeman's Journal*, 2 October 1906; Mary Gallagher, *16Lives: Éamonn Ceannt* (Dublin, 2014), p. 58.

33 Seamus Ua Caomhanaigh, BMH.WS0889, p. 34.

34 Harry C. Phibbs, BMH.WS0848, pp. 11–12; *Ulster Herald*, 26 August 1905; *Irish Independent*, 26 January 1906.

35 *Irish Independent*, 26 January 1906.

36 *Freeman's Journal*, 21 December 1908.

37 *The Kerryman*, 26 December 1908.

38 *Freeman's Journal*, 15 December 1906.

39 Seamus Ua Caomhanaigh, BMH.WS0889, pp. 16, 30.

40 House of Lord, Debates, 17 March 1903 (Hansard volume 119, column 986) available online http://hansard.millbanksystems.com/lords/1903/mar/17/bank-holidays-ireland-bill-second-reading. Accessed 23 June 2015.

41 Seamus Ua Caomhanaigh, BMH.WS0889, pp. 30–1.

42 *Irish Independent*, 13 March 1904; Ceannt-O'Brennan Papers MS 13,069/46.

43 Seamus Ua Caomhanaigh, BMH.WS0889, p. 27–8.

44 *Ibid*. p. 28.

45 Ceannt-O'Brennan Papers MS 13,069/26. For Henry, see *Freeman's Journal*, 9 March 1906.

46 TG McMahon, *Grand Opportunity: The Gaelic Revival and Irish Society, 1893–1910* (New York, 2008), p. 190; AJ Nolan, 'Phoenix Park Public Meetings', *Dublin Historical Record*, 14. 4 (1958), 102–113.

47 NLI MS 11536, Minutes of All Ireland Demonstration Committee, 10 September 1909.

48 *The Times,* 20 September 1909.

49 Seamus Ua Caomhanaigh, BMH.WS0889, p. 32–3.

50 *Freeman's Journal*, 31 October 1905.

51 *Freeman's Journal*, 27 December 1905.

52 *Freeman's Journal*, 4 January 1908.

53 *Freeman's Journal,* 28 September 1909.

Chapter 6

1 Harry C. Phibbs, BMH.WS0848, p. 11.

2 Francis P Jones, *History of the Sinn Féin Movement and the Irish Rebellion of 1916* (New York: 1917), p. 167.

3 Helen Litton, *16Lives: Tom Clarke* (Dublin, 2014), p. 85.

4 Stephen Brown, ed., *Ireland in Fiction* (Dublin, 1919), Vol 1. p. 204.

5 Other titles with this theme include Samuel Lover, *Treasure Trove* (Constable, 1844); Charles Graham Halpine (writing as Private Myles O'Reilly), *Mountcashel's Brigade* (TD Sullivan, 1882); William Carleton, *The Red-Haired Man's Wife* (Sealy, 1889); Sir Samuel R. Keightley, *The Last Recruit of Clare's* (Hutchinson, 1897); Robert White (writing as Owen Blayney), *The Macmahon* (Constable, 1898); GA Henty, *In the Irish Brigade* (Scribner, 1901); NW Knowles (writing as May Wynne), *For Charles the Rover* (Greening, 1909).

6 Michael O hAnnrachain, *A Swordsman of the Brigade* (Edinburgh, 1914), pp. 47–8.

7 *Ibid*. p. 206.

8 *Ibid*. pp. 191–2.

9 Thomas Johnson Collection. C.D. 258/2/9 Tadhg Barry, 54 Blarney St Cork, 1 October 1915.

10 O hAnnrachain, *A Swordsman of the Brigade* p. 71; p. 144.

11 Fr Michael O'Flanagan in Miceál Ua hAnnracáin, *Irish Heroines* (Dublin, 1917), p. 4.

12 TJ Meldon, BMH.WS734, p. 5.

13 *Irish Independent*, 29 August 1917.

14 *Irish Press*, 29 December 1941.

15 SJ Brown 'Irish Fiction for Boys', Studies (1919), 469–72.

16 *Irish Freedom*, January 1911.

17 Michael O'Hanrahan, *When the Norman Came* (Dublin, 1918), p. 59.

18 *Ibid*. pp. 11–12.

19 *Ibid*. p. 15.

20 Conor Kostick, review: Charles Townshend, 'Easter 1916: The Irish Rebellion', *Science & Society* (April, 2009), 73.2, 281–283.

21 *The Irish Volunteer*, Vol 2.52 (new series), 4 December 1915.

22 See, for example, Conor Kostick, *Strongbow* (Dublin, 2013).

23 Michael O'Hanrahan, *When the Norman Came* (Dublin, 1918), p. 132.

24 *Ibid*. p. 101.

25 *Ibid*. p. 79.

26 *Ibid*.

27 John M. Feehan, *My Village, My World* (Cork, 1992), p. 115.

28 Francis P Jones, *History of the Sinn Féin Movement and the Irish Rebellion of 1916* (New York, 1917), p. 167.

29 Miceál Ua hAnnracáin, *Irish Heroines* (Dublin, 1917), p. 9.

30 *Ibid*. pp. 10–11.

31 *Ibid*. pp. 20–1.

32 *Ibid*. pp. 26–7.

33 *Ibid*. p. 30.

34 Eily O'Hanrahan O'Reilly, BMH.WS0270, p. 10.

35 Eily left no will, but she was survived by her husband Thomas A O'Reilly and nieces and nephews in Limerick, Dundalk, Carlow, New Ross, Wexford and Dublin. If someone has the manuscript, I would encourage him or her to bring its contents into the public domain, for example, by contacting the National Library in the first instance.

Chapter 7

1 http://www.census.nationalarchives.ie/reels/nai000036280/ accessed 25 June 2014.

2 http://www.census.nationalarchives.ie/pages/1911/Dublin/Glasnevin/Connaught_Street/9021/ accessed 25 June 2014.

3 http://www.nival.ie/collections/collections/collection/archive/mrs-eily-o-hanrahan-o-rielly/view/item. Accessed 25 June 2014.

4 Eily O'Hanrahan O'Reilly, BMH.WS0270, p. 2.

5 *The Irish Volunteer,* Vol 1.39, 31 October 1914.

6 Seán T O'Kelly, BMH.WS1765, p. 128.

7 http://www.nationalarchives.ie/digital-resources/chief-secretarys-office-crime-branch-dublin-metropolitan-police-dmp-movement-of-extremists-29-may-1915-20-april-1916/. Accessed 11 June 2015.

8 See also Seamus Ua Caomhanaigh, BMH.WS0889, p. 40.

9 Gearoid Ua h-Uallachain, BMH.WS0328, p. 48. Seamus Daly, BMH.WS0360, pp. 14.

10 Daniel Dennehy, BMH.WS0116.

11 Thomas Johnson Collection. C.D. 258/2/22.

12 Seán T. O'Kelly, BMH.WS1765, p. 128, p. 129.

13 Liam Tannam, BMH.WS0242, pp. 6–7. See also Eily O'Hanrahan O'Reilly, BMH.WS0270, p. 1; Kitty O'Doherty, BMH.WS0355, pp. 5–6.

14 Right Rev Monsignor M. Curran, P.P, BMH.WS0687, p.26.

15 Kitty O'Doherty, BMH.WS0355, pp. 5–6.

16 Gearoid Ua h-Uallachain, BMH.WS0328, p. 48.

17 TJ Meldon, BMH.WS0734, p. 10.

18 Liam Tannam, BMH.WS0242, p. 5.

19 Seamus Kavanagh, BMH.WS0208, p. 5.

20 Robert Holland, BMH.WS0280, p. 8.

21 Liam O'Carroll, BMH 314, p. 5.

22 Sean Murphy, BMH.WS0204, p. 4.

23 John MacDonagh [brother of Thomas], BMH.WS0532, p. 3.

24 Frank McGrath, BMH.WS1558, p. 2.

25 Thomas Johnson Collection. C.D. 258/2/8.

26 Pat McCartan, BMH.WS0766, p. 35.

27 Francis P Jones, *History of the Sinn Féin Movement and the Irish Rebellion of 1916* (New York: 1917), p. 167.

28 Seamus Ua Caomhanaigh, BMH.WS0889, p. 40.

29 Seamus Daly, BMH.WS0360, pp. 16–17.

30 Seamus Daly, BMH.WS0360, pp. 18–19.

31 Aine Heron, BMH.WS0293, p. 1.

32 Maire O'Brolchain, BMH.WS0321, p. 5.

33 Seosamh Ua Ruairc, BHM.WS1244, p. 5; Eily O'Hanrahan, BMH.WS0270, p. 2.

34 Patrick Egan, BMH.WS0327, pp. 9–10.

35 Michael Walker, BMH.WS0139, p.5.

36 *United Ireland*, 6 June 1936.

37 *Irish Press*, 20 June 1936.

38 Michael Staines, BMH.WS0274, p. 4; Michael Staines, BMH.WS0944, p. 24.

39 Seamus Daly, BMH.WS0360, pp. 19–20.

40 Liam Tannam, BMH.WS0242, p. 7.

41 John MacDonagh [brother of Thomas], BMH.WS0532, p.2.

42 Liam Tannam, BMH.WS0242, p. 7.

43 Jeremiah Joseph O'Leary, BMH.WS1108, p. 10.

44 Eily O'Hanrahan O'Reilly, BMH.WS 0270, p. 9.

45 Joseph McCarthy, BMH.WS1497, pp. 12–13.

46 Seumas Kavanagh, 1670, BMH.WS1670, p. 15.

47 Eily O'Hanrahan O'Reilly, BMH.WS0270, p. 2.

48 Eily O'Hanrahan O'Reilly, BMH.WS0270, p. 2.

49 Seumas Kavanagh, 1670, BMH.WS1670, p. 27.

50 http://mspcsearch.militaryarchives.ie/docs/files//PDF_Pensions/
   R1/1D445MichaelOHanrahan/WF523MichaelOHanrahan.pdf

Chapter 8

1 TJ Meldon, BMH.WS0734, p. 15.

2 Liam Tannam, BMH.WS0242, pp. 6–7.

3 Donal O'Hanigan, BMH.WS0161, pp. 33–4.

4 Robert Holland, BMH.WS0280, p. 8.

5 Thomas Johnson Collection. C.D. 258/2/22.

6 Eily O'Hanrahan, BMH.WS0270, p. 3.

7 Gregory Murphy, BMH.WS0150, p. 5.

8 Seumas Kavanagh, 1670, BMH.WS1670, p. 28.

9 Eily O'Hanrahan, BMH.WS0270, pp. 4–5.

10 Kitty O'Doherty, Quartermaster Cumann na mBan 1916, WS 355, pp. 8–9.

11 William James Stapleton, BMH.WS0822, p. 3.

12 Liam Tannam, BMH.WS0242, pp. 8–9.

13 James Grace, BMW.WS0310, p. 3.

14 Eily O'Hanrahan O'Reilly, BMH.WS0270, pp. 2–3.

15 Eily O'Hanrahan O'Reilly, BMH.WS0270, p. 5.

16 Rose McNamara, BMH.WS0482, p. 3.

17 Gearoid Ua h-Uallachain, BMH.WS0328, p. 50.

18 Gearoid Ua h-Uallachain, BMH.WS0328, p. 53.

19 Kitty O'Doherty, BMH.WS0355, pp. 21–2.

20 Jeremiah Joseph O'Leary, BMH.WS1108, p. 10.

21 Seumas Kavanagh, BMH.WS1670, p. 29.

22 Seumas Kavanagh, BMH.WS1670, p. 30.

23 Frank Henderson, BMH.WS0249, p. 27.

24 Peg Conlon, BMH.WS0419, p. 6.

25 Peadar Mac Cana, BMH.WS0171, p.3.

26 Seamus Daly, BMH.WS0360, p. 24.

27 Cathleen McCarthy, BMH.WS0937, p. 4.

28 Seamus Ua Caomhanaigh, BMH.WS0889, p. 44.

29 Kitty O'Doherty, BMH.WS0355, p. 26.

30 Richard Hayes, BMH.WS0097, p.3

31 Eily O'Hanrahan O'Reilly, BMH.WS0270, pp. 5–6.

32 Seumas Kavanagh, BMH.WS1670, p. 32; John MacDonagh, BHM.WS0532, p. 10.

33 Seumas Kavanagh, BMH.WS1670, p. 32. Also, TJ Meldon, BMH.WS0734, p. 22.

34 Seumas Kavanagh, BMH.WS1670, p. 34.

35 TJ Meldon, BMH.WS0734, p. 22.

36 John MacDonagh, BHM.WS0532, p. 10.

37 www.nationalarchives.ie/topics/1916/jacobschapter.html. Accessed 27 September 2014.

38 *The Kerryman*, 9 April 1966.

39 Eily O'Hanrahan O'Reilly, BMH.WS0270, p. 8.

40 *Ibid*.

41 *Ibid*.

42 TJ Meldon, BMH.WS0734, p. 24.

43 Joseph Furlong BMH.WS0335 p. 8.

44 Séamas Ó Maitiú, *W&R Jacob: Celebrating 150 Years of Irish Biscuit Making* (Dublin, 2001). Quoted at http://www.nationalarchives.ie/topics/1916/jacobschapter.html. Accessed 1 October 2014; Thomas Pugh, BMH.WS0397, p. 4.

45 Patrick Rankin, BMH.WS0163, p. 9.

46 Seosamh de Brun, BMH.WS0312, p. 8.

47 Séamas Ó Maitiú, W&R Jacob.

48 Diarmud Lynch, BMH.WS0120, p. 5.

49 Seosamh de Brun, BMH.WS0312, p. 8.

50 Seosamh de Brun, BMH.WS0312, *passim*.

51 Seosamh de Brun, BMH.WS0312, pp. 14–15; Charles O'Grady, BMH.WS0282, p. 7; Joseph Furlong, BMH.WS0335, p. 7.

52 John MacDonagh, BHM.WS0532, p. 13; Fr Aloysius, OFM, Cap., 'Personal Recollections', Capuchin Annual (1966).

53 Bob Price, BMH.WS995, p. 1.

54 *Ibid*. p. 2.

55 Thomas Pugh, BMH.WS039, p. 6.

56 Seosamh de Brun, BMH.WS0312, p. 18.

57 Joseph Furlong, BMH.WS0335 pp. 7–8.

58 Padraig O'Kelly, BMH.WS0376, p. 4.

59 Fr Michael O'Flanagan in Miceál Ua hAnnracáin, *Irish Heroines* (Dublin, 1917), p. 4.

60 Eily O'Hanrahan, BMH.WS0270, pp. 15.

61 Bob Price, BMH.WS995, pp. 2–3; Thomas Pugh, BMH.WS039, p. 7.

Chapter 9

1 Thomas Pugh, BMH.WS039, p. 7.

2 *Ibid*.; William O'Brien, BMH.WS1766, p. 14.

3 Joseph V Lawless, BMH.WS1043, pp. 139–41.

4 Eamon Broy, WS 1280, pp. 50–1.

5 Seumas Kavanagh, 1670, BMH.WS1670, pp. 44–5.

6 William O'Brien, BMH.WS1766, p. 14.

7 http://dh.tcd.ie/letters1916/diyhistory/scripto/transcribe/740/1929, accessed 7 October 2014.

8 http://dh.tcd.ie/letters1916/diyhistory/scripto/transcribe/701/1924.

9 PRO W071/357 quoted in Brian Barton, *From Behind a Closed Door: The Secret Court Martial Records of the 1916 Easter Rising* (Belfast, 2002), p. 180.

10 Maxwell memorandum, 11 May 1916, Asquith Papers MS43/26-33, Bodleian Library, Oxford University, quoted in *Brian Barton, From Behind a Closed Door: The Secret Court Martial Records of the 1916 Easter Rising* (Belfast, 2002), p. 176.

11 Sir Reginald Bade, quoted in *Brian Barton, From Behind a Closed Door: The Secret Court Martial Records of the 1916 Easter Rising* (Belfast, 2002), p. 178.

12 Eily O'Hanrahan, BMH.WS0270, pp. 10–12.

13 Francis P Jones, *History of the Sinn Féin Movement and the Irish Rebellion of 1916* (New York: 1917) p. 418.

14 http://dh.tcd.ie/letters1916/diyhistory/scripto/transcribe/680/1676. Accessed 7 October 2014.

15 *The Nationalist and Leinster Times*, 8 May 1916; 20 May 1916. My thanks to Michael Purcell for this information.

16 Fr Augustine, BMH.WS0920, p. 21.

17 Aine Bean E. Ceannt, BMH.WS0264, p. 38.

18 Liam Tannam, BMH.WS0242, p. 45.

Chapter 10

1 Fr Augustine, BMH.WS0920, p. 22.

2 *Ibid.*

3 *Irish Press*, 5 May 1966.

4 http://dh.tcd.ie/letters1916/diyhistory/scripto/transcribe/999/2572. Accessed 7 October 2014.

5 *Thom's* Directory, 1915; Eily O'Hanrahan, WS 0415, p. 3; Eily O'Hanrahan, BMH. WS0270, p. 16.

6 *Ibid.* p. 17.

7 Sean Prendergast, WS. 755, p. 563; *Irish Independent*, 13 January 1922.

8 *Freeman's Journal*, 20 July 1922.

9 Eilis Ni Conaill (nee Eilis ni Riain), http://mspcsearch.militaryarchives.ie/docs/files/PDF_Pensions/R1/1D445MichaelOHanrahan/WF523MichaelOHanrahan.pdf. Accessed 10 October 2014; Eily O'Hanrahan, BMH.WS0270, p. 16.

10 Eily O'Hanrahan, BMH.WS0270, p. 17.

11 Military Service Pensions Collection, Eily O'Hanrahan, MSP34REF17180. Available at http://mspcsearch.militaryarchives.ie/detail.aspx?parentpriref=. Accessed 15 October 2014.

12 Eamon Broy, BMH.WS1280, pp. 58, 69–72.

13 Eamon Broy, BMH.WS1280, p. 58.

14 Eamon Broy, BMW.WS1284, p.1; BMH.WS1285, p. 22.

15 Military Service Pensions Collection, DP25774, Henry O'Hanrahan, available at http://mspcsearch.militaryarchives.ie/detail.aspx?parentpriref=. Accessed 15 October 2014.

16 Eily O'Hanrahan, BMH.WS0415, p. 4.

17 Military Service Pensions Collection, Eily O'Hanrahan, MSP34REF17180. Available at http://mspcsearch.militaryarchives.ie/detail.aspx?parentpriref=. Accessed 15 October 2014.

18 *Manchester Guardian*, 2 February 1920.

19 *Sunday Independent*, 14 March 1920.

20 See Conor Kostick, *Revolution in Ireland* (Cork, 2009), pp. 129–139.

21 Eamon O'Duibhir, BMH.WS1474, pp. 74–5.

22 Sean Matthews BMH.WS1022. pp. 10–11.

23 *Skibbereen Eagle,* 8 April 1922; *Southern Star,* 8 April 1922.

24 Military Service Pensions Collection, Eily O'Hanrahan, MSP34REF17180. Available at http://mspcsearch.militaryarchives.ie/detail.aspx?parentpriref=. Accessed 15 October 2014.

25 For the background to the strike, see Conor Kostick, *Revolution in Ireland*, pp. 199–200.

26 *Connacht Tribune* 23 September 1922; *Irish Independent* 16 September 1922; *Irish Independent* 23 September 1922.

27 Military Service Pensions Collection, Henry O'Hanrahan, DP25774. Available at http://mspcsearch.militaryarchives.ie/detail.aspx?parentpriref=. Accessed 15 October 2014; *Irish Press*, 1 October 1932.

28 *Irish Press*, 17 June 1937.

29 Military Service Pensions Collection, DP25774, Henry O'Hanrahan, available at http://mspcsearch.militaryarchives.ie/detail.aspx?parentpriref=. Accessed 15 October 2014.

30 Military Service Pensions Collection, Henry O'Hanrahan, DP25774. Available at http://mspcsearch.militaryarchives.ie/detail.aspx?parentpriref=. Accessed 15 October 2014.

31 Military Service Pensions Collection, Eily O'Hanrahan, MSP34REF17180. Available at http://mspcsearch.militaryarchives.ie/detail.aspx?parentpriref=. Accessed 15 October 2014.

32 Desmond Ryan, BMH.WS0275, p. 10.

Index